How to Select & Grow

AFRICAN VIOLETS

AND OTHER GESNERIADS

by Theodore James Jr.

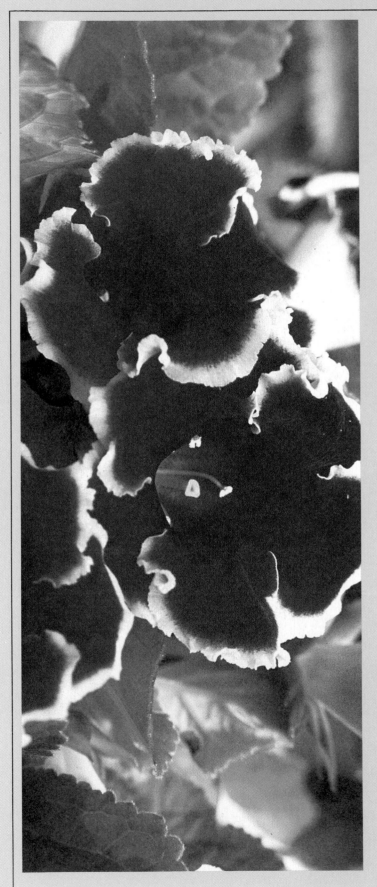

HPBooks

Publishers
Bill and Helen Fisher

Executive Editor
Rick Bailey

Editorial Director
Randy Summerlin

Editor
Scott Millard

Art Director
Don Burton

Book Design
Kathleen Koopman

Photography
Harry Haralambou

Illustrations
Doug Burton

Cover Photo
'Hawaii' Optimara
by Harry Haralambou

About the Author

Theodore James Jr. is a dedicated grower of African violets who raises fruit, vegetables and flowers as well. He is the author of 10 other books, including the HPBook, *Fruit, Berries and Nuts for the Midwest and East*. He is a regular contributor of horticultural articles to the *New York Times* and several national magazines. James gardens at his home on the north fork of Long Island, New York.

Acknowledgments

The author wishes to thank the following individuals and organizations for their cooperation and assistance:

Albert and Diantha Buell, Buell's Greenhouses Inc., Eastport, CT

Ms. Anne C. Crowley, American Gloxinia and Gesneriad Society, New Milford, CT

Mrs. Sandra Dobie, North Star African Violet Society, Huntington, NY

Leila Egenites, Annalee Violetry, Bayside, NY

Charles W. Fischer Jr., Fischer Greenhouses, Linwood, NJ

Schneider Greenhouses, Cutchogue, NY

Reinhold Holtkamp, Hermann Holtkamp Greenhouses, Nashville, TN

Michael MacCaskey, St. Helena, CA

New York State African Violet Society

George W. Park Seed Co., Greenwood, SC

Riverhead New York Free Public Library, Riverhead, NY

The African Violet Company, Greenwood, SC

Mrs. Sandy Weynand, Weynand Greenhouse, East Moriches, NY

Mrs. Alma Wright, Knoxville, TN

Contents

Queen of House Plants 5

African Violet Basics 9
  Soil or Planting Medium 10
  Pots and Potting 13
  Light 16
  Water 20
  Temperature, Humidity and Ventilation . 23
  Fertilizer 26
  Pests and Diseases 28

Propagating Plants 35
  Creating Hybrids 41

Displaying & Showing African Violets 45
  Showtime 50

Encyclopedia of African Violets 55
  Standard Varieties 57
  Miniatures and Semiminiatures 108
  Trailing Varieties 110

African Violet Relatives 113
  Lesser-Known Gesneriads 138

Glossary 140

Sources 141

Index 142

Published by HPBooks
P.O. Box 5367
Tucson, AZ 85703
602/888-2150
ISBN: 0-89586-222-0
Library of Congress Catalog Card Number: 83-81327
© 1983 Fisher Publishing Inc.
Printed in U.S.A.

Queen of House Plants

African violets are among the most well-known house plants in the world. Plants are attractive and grow in a variety of sizes and shapes, from miniatures a few inches high to trailing forms that drape from pots. But the flowers of African violets are what make them so appealing. Colors range from white to pink, burgundy, wine, fuchsia, blue, deep purple and striking combinations. Foliage is lush and multishaped in various shades of green.

African violets are attractive additions to your home decor. Use them to fill a window with color. Grown under lights, they brighten dark corners. Place plants wherever a touch of greenery or a splash of color is desired.

Despite their reputation as being fussy plants, African violets thrive with minimum care. They are bothered by few pests and diseases. Because they are easy to propagate, African violets are great for the hobbyist and collector. Many growers that began with one or two plants now have a hundred!

African violets belong to the *Gesneriaceae* family, genus *Saintpaulia*. They are common-ly referred to as *gesneriads*. In this book, we will call *Saintpaulia* species by their common name, African violets. There are 27 known species of *Saintpaulia*. Other gesneriads such as *Columnea* and *Sinningia* are discussed in African Violet Relatives, pages 113 to 139. These gesneriads generally require the same cultivation and propagation techniques as African violets.

Read this book carefully, paying close attention to the chapter on African Violet Basics. The information is presented in simple, easy-to-follow terms for the beginning grower. In addition, specialized techniques such as how to hybridize plants are provided for experienced hobbyists. Learning the proper methods of potting and caring for plants will guide you to success.

Use the Encyclopedia of African Violets on pages 55 to 111 to help you make your plant selections. It contains photographs and descriptions of more than 100 varieties. These allow you to compare plant form, foliage and flower color to determine the varieties you want to grow.

This book can help you join the millions of gardeners throughout the world who enjoy growing African violets and other gesneriads.

Left: Blossoms of African violets come in more than traditional violet-color hues. These plants in a commercial greenhouse represent a small sample of the many colors available. Above: 'Delaware' cultivar has a striking simplicity, representing part of the appeal of African violets.

Because there are thousands of varieties to choose from, African violets are great for the collector. Ideas for displaying plants are shown on pages 45 to 49.

A BIT OF HISTORY

In 1892, Baron von Saint Paul was serving as the imperial district governor of Tanganyika, now Tanzania, a small country in east Africa. The Baron discovered and collected two of the plants now called *African violets*. He sent seeds of these plants to his father in Germany. His father was impressed with their delicate beauty, and took them to the Royal Botanical Garden at Herrenhausen, Germany. Hermann Wendland, botanist and director of the Royal Botanical Garden, gave the plants their botanical name: *Saintpaulia ionantha*. The genus name, *Saintpaulia,* was named after the Baron. The species name, *ionantha,* is Greek for "resembling a violet," in reference to the flower.

During the early years of the 20th century, African violets were grown only in botanical gardens or conservatories on large estates. It wasn't until 1926 that plants were introduced commercially to the United States. Growers began experimenting by crossing varieties to create 'Admiral', 'Amethyst', 'Blue Boy', 'Commodore' and 'Neptune'. These early hybrids, offspring produced by crossing two different plant varieties, are still popular today.

As more people began growing African violets, *mutants* began to appear. These are plants with variations differing markedly from their parent plants. Variations are caused by changes in genes or chromosomes. If the mutants had attractive features, they were propagated. The thousands of African violet varieties now available are the result of hybridization and mutations.

Yellow, orange or crimson-red African violets are yet to be produced. Extensive genetic experiments with hybrids and radiation treatments may produce plants with these colors in the future.

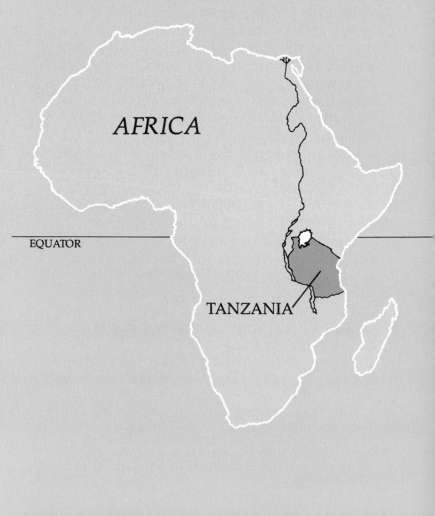

AFRICA

EQUATOR

TANZANIA

Gloxinia, like the African violet, is a *gesneriad*—member of the *Gesneriaceae* family. Large, velvety, bell-shape flowers come in a range of colors, including red, purple, blue and white. Culture for gloxinias and most gesneriads is the same as for African violets. For more information on African violet relatives, see pages 113 to 139.

African violets are commonly grown under fluorescent lights. Because you control intensity and duration of light, blooms can be grown to perfection.

African Violet Basics

T his chapter contains information on how to plant and grow African violets and other gesneriads. Soil, potting, light, water, fertilizer, temperature and humidity requirements, and identifying and treating plant problems are discussed.

Some people consider African violets and other gesneriads to be fragile plants. But they are among the easiest house plants to grow. With minimum care, they will grow and bloom. However, without proper attention to cultural needs, their full potential will not be realized. Only regular care will produce plants with spectacular bloom and vigorous health.

Follow these basics for success:
● Use a commercially produced African violet soil mix, available at most garden centers. An African violet mix contains lightweight, porous materials for good drainage. Do not use a house-plant potting soil. It does not have the good drainage or pH level required by African violets.
● Select pots that have drainage holes so excess water can drain from soil. Roots of African violets are shallow and will not fill the depth of a standard pot. Pots that are slightly squat, called *bulb* or *pan-type* pots, are preferred over standard pots.
● Grow plants in bright light but not direct

Left: Few basic tools and materials are required to grow African violets. They include pots and potting soil, watering implements and fertilizer. Scissors and tweezers are used to keep plants groomed. Above: Bottom watering is one of several ways to provide plants with regular moisture.

sunlight, except during short days of winter.
● Provide plants with about 12 to 14 hours of bright, indirect light each day. If growing plants under fluorescent light, provide about 14 hours each day.
● Overwatering causes more plant failure than any other factor. Water only after checking to see if the top 1/2 inch of soil surface in the pot is dry. Water plants with room-temperature water.
● Isolate new plants for at least one month before adding them to your collection. If new plants host pests or diseases, you will notice them before your healthy plants are infected.
● Provide proper temperatures and humidity. Ideal temperatures are 72F to 75F (22C to 24C) during the day and 67F to 70F (20C to 21C) at night. Maintain humidity levels as close as possible to 40% to 60%. Give plants good air circulation, but keep them out of drafts.
● Fertilize plants regularly with African violet fertilizer, or use organic fertilizer such as fish emulsion. Switch types of fertilizers occasionally to avoid buildup of fertilizer salts in the soil.
● Keep plants clean and tidy, and inspect plants regularly. Remove all spent flowers, leaves and stems.

African violets require light, porous, well-draining soil.

African violets and other gesneriads adapt to a wide variety of soil types and mixtures. In their natural habitat, African violets grow in leaf litter in crevices of limestone cliffs. Several mixes work well. They include *African violet mixes* sold in packages, *soilless mixes* and *homemade mixes*. All are discussed in the following. Whichever medium you choose, African violets grow best in soil having these qualities:

Loose, Porous Texture—This allows good penetration of air and water. A loose mix will crumble in your hand when gently squeezed.

Good Drainage—Mix should allow plant to retain water necessary for growth, while excess water drains through soil and out of pot.

Sterilized or Pasteurized—Mixtures are usually treated with heat or chemicals to destroy harmful pests and diseases. The terms *sterilize* and *pasteurize* are often used interchangeably, but most soil mixes are pasteurized—treated at 180F (83C)—to kill plant-disease bacteria, plant viruses, soil insects and most weed seeds. Heating soil above 180F (83C) kills beneficial bacteria. Even if package label says it is sterilized or pasteurized, it is a good idea to pasteurize soil yourself before using. This is especially true if propagating plants from seeds or cuttings. See page 12 for instructions.

High Percentage of Organic Matter—These would include vegetative particles such as peat moss or compost. These retain water, yet make the soil mix porous to allow for necessary drainage.

SOIL pH

pH is a term you should understand when selecting and maintaining a proper growing medium for any plant. African violets are no exception. Soil pH refers to the relative levels of *acidity* or *alkalinity* in the soil. All plants have a preference, whether it is neutral, acid or alkaline. Acid soils are rich in decaying organic or vegetative matter. This decaying matter forms dilute acid. Alkaline soils are the opposite, containing little or no acid-releasing decaying matter.

Commercial African violet mixes differ from commercial house-plant potting mixes. African violet mixes are generally more porous and have better drainage. But more important, the soil pH in African violet mixes is slightly more acidic than house-plant potting soil.

Test kits and electric meters that measure pH are available at nurseries or plant-supply stores. You can also have your soil tested by a professional soil-test laboratory. Most state universities will test your soil for a fee. Contact the nearest state university or your cooperative extension service for more information.

The soil pH for African violets and other gesneriads should be between 6.4 and 7.0. If soil is alkaline—above 7.0 on the pH scale—soak soil with a solution of 2 tablespoons white vinegar to 1 gallon water.

If soil is acidic—below 6.4 on the pH scale—add dolomite lime. Do not use quick-acting hydrated lime.

It will burn plant roots. Start by adding 2-1/2 tablespoons per 1/2 bushel of soil mixture. Mix thoroughly and test. If the soil is still too acidic, add another tablespoon of lime, mix and test again.

The pH factor in commercial African violet mixtures is usually correct. If you make your own mix, it is a good idea to test soil pH before potting plants.

SOIL MIXTURES

Commercially produced African violet soil mixes are perfectly suited and recommended for African violets and other gesneriads. Dozens of products labeled "African Violet Soil Mix" or similar are available. Most commercial mixes have good drainage and porous texture necessary for African violets.

Commercial mixes arc recommended over other growing mediums. They are convenient, economical and contain the proper balance of nutrient elements necessary for growth. They are available in most supermarkets, garden centers, nurseries and discount stores.

Most mixes are pasteurized—heated to 180F (82C). They contain proper combinations of organic and nonorganic materials for loose, porous texture. Garden soil, peat moss, leaf mold or compost are also included in mixes. They help create the proper acid content.

Before potting plants, give the soil mixture a quick check. Grab a handful and feel it. If the soil is heavy—not loose or porous—drainage may be poor. You can improve drainage by adding *perlite,* a lightweight, volcanic product. Or add *horticultural vermiculite,* a mica product. Both vermiculite and perlite are sterile and available in packages at garden centers and nurseries. How much to add depends on the nature of the mix. As a guide, add 1 part vermiculite or perlite to 3 parts soil.

House-plant potting soil straight from the bag is usually not porous and loose enough in texture for African violets. It can be used as an ingredient in homemade mixes. See page 12.

SOILLESS MEDIUM OR MIXES

Many growers use soilless mixes. They are termed soilless because they do not contain natural soil from outdoors. Texture is loose, with high porosity and good drainage necessary for successful African violet culture. Ingredients are sterilized.

Soilless mixes usually contain sphagnum peat moss and sand, or horticultural vermiculite or perlite and a small amount of African violet fertilizer. Soilless mixes contain no natural mineral nutrients. Regular applications of a weak fertilizer solution will be necessary. Many growers fertilize with each watering.

One recommended soilless mixture is:
- 2 quarts sphagnum peat moss
- 1 quart horticultural vermiculite
- 1 quart perlite
- 1 tablespoon ground dolomite limestone

Mix ingredients the same as recommended in Making Your Own Soil Mix, page 12.

Soil and Plant Growth

African violets require a loose, porous planting medium, such as an African violet soil mix. This allows good distribution of water and nutrients to plant roots. Loose, porous mix also drains well, so air, necessary for roots to live and grow, can reach the root zone. Spaces between particles that make up the mix retain water and fertilizer solution for a short time. They can then be absorbed by tiny root hairs and distributed to plant.

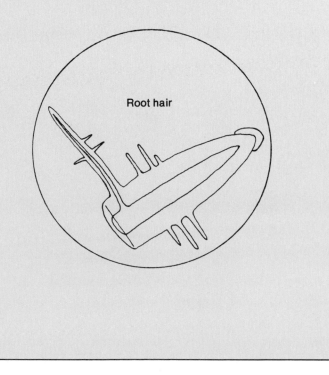

Root hair

MAKING YOUR OWN SOIL MIX

Many African violet growers make their own soil mixtures. The recipes for mixes are almost as numerous as there are gardeners. Here is one of the easiest to make that satisfies the requirements of African violets.

- 1 part commercial house-plant potting soil
- 1 part sphagnum peat moss
- 1 part horticultural vermiculite or perlite

Place all ingredients in container. A large, clean, plastic trash barrel treated with a bleach and water solution—1 part bleach to 10 parts water—works well. Mix them together thoroughly with your hands or large spoon. Keep ingredients dry if you are storing the mix. If you plan to pot right away, moisten the mix you will use.

Experts at Cornell University in Ithaca, New York, recommend the following mixture for African violets. Use a 6-inch pot to measure ingredients. To make 1/2 bushel combine:

- 4-1/2 pots shredded, unspoiled imported sphagnum peat moss
- 2-1/4 pots horticultural vermiculite, grade 2 or 3
- 2-1/4 pots perlite, medium grade
- 2-1/2 tablespoons dolomite limestone
- 1-1/4 tablespoons 20% superphosphate
- 3-3/4 tablespoons 5-10-5 or 6-12-6 all-purpose fertilizer
- 1 quart *Peters Soluble Trace Element* from solution. To make the solution, add 1/4 teaspoon to 1 gallon of water.

PASTEURIZING MIXES

If you make your own soil mix, pasteurize all ingredients. This will avoid soil-borne problems with pests and diseases. Pasteurization is different from sterilization in that it destroys certain pathogenic organisms and undesirable bacteria. Substances are heated to 180F (83C). If temperatures go over 180F (83C), beneficial soil bacteria are killed.

To pasteurize a soil mixture, fill a large roasting pan with mix. Moisten with hot water. Cover with aluminum foil and insert a meat thermometer through foil into mix. Place in oven and set temperature at 180F (83C). Check meat thermometer frequently. When temperature registers 180F (83C), bake mixture for 1 hour. Do not allow temperature to go over 180F (83C). Take pan out of oven. Remove cover and allow mix to air for at least four days before use. Stir several times each day to increase aeration.

Chemical Treatment—Products are available at nurseries and garden centers that can be used to pasteurize soil. Use these as instructed by the manufacturer. Generally, you soak planting medium with a liquid solution. The liquid kills unwanted organisms and bacteria. As with soils pasteurized by baking, do not use treated soil for four days after treatment. Check the product label to be sure. Stir soil during this period.

Storing Mixes—To keep soil mix free of pests and diseases, store in a container that has been treated with a bleach and water solution.

African violet soil mix, left, is lighter in weight and more porous than house-plant potting soil, right. This provides African violets with fast drainage and air in the soil, necessary for proper growth.

POTS AND POTTING

Pots, planters and baskets from a garden center represent wide selection of containers available for African violets.

Dozens of kinds of pots and containers are available for African violet plants. Plastic, glazed and unglazed clay pots, hanging baskets made from wire frames and sphagnum moss, and glass terrariums are some of the more common. Each type has advantages and disadvantages.

Most African violets are grown in clay or plastic pots. Growers cannot agree which type is best. Experienced African violet and gesneriad growers usually recommend plastic pots. They prefer them because they are lightweight, easy to handle and keep clean. Because they are not porous, plastic pots retain more moisture than clay. The rims of plastic pots stay relatively dry. Pot rims that are constantly moist can promote stem and leaf rot. Because plastic pots are airtight, it is important to keep soil loose at top of pot so air can enter. Dig top layer of soil with a fork to prevent it from crusting over. Do not dig too deep or you may damage roots. See illustration, page 14.

Some gardeners prefer clay pots for their natural appearance. If you choose to grow plants in clay, be aware of the difference between *glazed* and *unglazed* pots. Glazed pots have a glossy, outer surface and are not porous. They retain moisture much like plastic pots. Unglazed clay pots are porous and permit evaporation of moisture. If African violets are overwatered, excess moisture has a chance to evaporate through the sides of the pot. For this reason, plants are less prone to develop root rot and crown rot. The pot's porous texture also allows increased air circulation around roots inside the pot.

If possible, plant all your plants in one kind of pot. This will simplify your watering schedule. If you have different pot types, the water needs of your plants will vary. Plants in plastic pots generally require about one-third of the water required by plants in unglazed clay pots.

POT SHAPE AND SIZE

African violets and other gesneriads have shallow roots. Because of this, squat, bulb-pan-type pots make better use of the soil than standard-shape pots.

Pots are graded by size in inches measured across the diameter of the top rim. Normal sizes for African violets are 2-1/4 inches, 3 inches, 4 inches and up to 6 inches for vigorous, mature plants. Height of pot is usually three-fourths the diameter. Plants do best if they fit the pot snugly. If the pot is too large for plant roots, foliage will be lush and healthy, but there will be little bloom. Plant energy goes into root and foliage growth in an attempt to fill pot.

DRAINAGE HOLES

Pots manufactured for use in growing house plants usually have a drainage hole or holes in the bottom. Drainage holes are necessary. If a pot does not allow water to drain, water will accumulate around the roots, forcing out air. Without air, the roots and plant will die.

If you have a container that does not have a drainage hole, it can still be used. Plant the African violet in a plastic or clay pot that has holes, and place it inside the container. Disguise this arrangement by covering over the inside container with a mulch of peat moss, bark chips or stones.

PREPARING POTS BEFORE PLANTING

New clay pots should be soaked in water overnight before you pot plants in them. This leaches out chemical substances that remain from the manufacturing process. Soaking also primes the pot by filling the porous clay with water. New plastic pots do not require treatment.

Clay and plastic pots that have been used previously may harbor insects or diseases that could infest your new plants. Place pots in boiling water for about 5 minutes to sterilize them. After boiling, soak in a solution of 1 part household bleach to 10 parts water. Scrub pots with hot, soapy water and a stiff brush to remove fertilizer salts, algae and dirt. Rinse pots thoroughly with clear water.

TRANSPLANTING

If a plant is *rootbound*—roots filling soil and coiling in the pot—it is time to transplant to a bigger pot. If plant has a poor general appearance and is getting rangy, it probably needs a larger home.

African violets thrive in a tight pot, but develop a *trunk*—an extended crown—if they become too rootbound. When potting rootbound African violets, bury this trunk to the level of the lowest leaves.

It is a good idea to check roots of *mature* plants once a year to see if they are rootbound. The best time to do this is in spring. Scrape loose soil from pot and clean pot. Plant with fresh soil mix.

Before removing rootbound plant from pot, water thoroughly. Soil and roots will cling in a mass, making the rootball easier to handle and reducing root damage during the process. Turn pot upside down and support soil in the palm of your hand. Gently tap the pot base with your other hand. Plant should slip from pot. If not, run a knife around inside edge of pot. Plant and rootball should come loose.

While the rootball is out of the pot, inspect the root system. If it appears as a loose mass of fine, white roots, the present pot size is correct. Plant in same pot or different pot of the same size, using fresh soil mix. If rootball appears as a tightly packed mass of white string, the plant is rootbound. Plant in a larger container. For step-by-step instructions, see page 15.

The new pot should be *one size* larger than the current pot. For example, if the plant was growing in a 2-1/4-inch pot, plant in a 3-inch pot. If the plant was in a 3-inch pot, plant in a 4-inch pot. This is true to a point. Generally, the largest pot for an African violet is a 6-inch pot. Other gesneriads may require slightly larger pots when mature, depending on the species and growing conditions.

Clay or Plastic Pots?

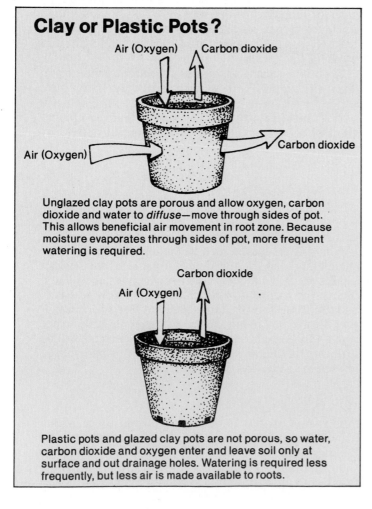

Unglazed clay pots are porous and allow oxygen, carbon dioxide and water to *diffuse*—move through sides of pot. This allows beneficial air movement in root zone. Because moisture evaporates through sides of pot, more frequent watering is required.

Plastic pots and glazed clay pots are not porous, so water, carbon dioxide and oxygen enter and leave soil only at surface and out drainage holes. Watering is required less frequently, but less air is made available to roots.

Pot Within a Pot

Containers that do not have drainage holes can be used to grow African violets and other house plants by planting a pot within a pot. Place activated charcoal in bottom of container, then place plant potted in container that has drainage holes inside. Fill area between pots with moss or perlite. Disguise arrangement by covering top of pot with a mulch of pebbles, peat moss or bark chips.

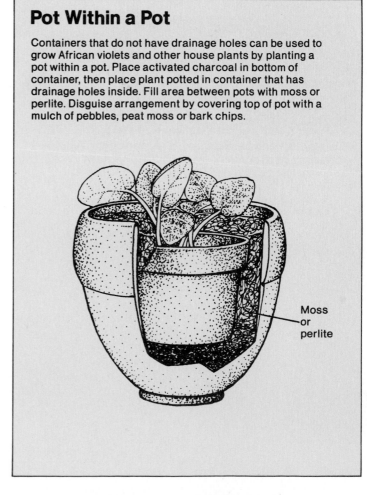

Moss or perlite

Potting African Violets Step by Step

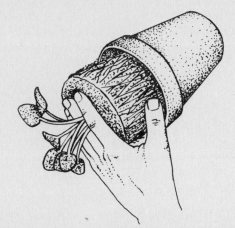

1. Cover drainage hole of new pot with broken crockery or fiberglass screening to keep planting medium from washing out during watering. Fill pot about one-third full with medium.

2. Thoroughly water plant to make removal easier. Invert pot in your hand, supporting plant and soil. Gently rap base of pot with your other hand and remove rootball.

Roots OK   Rootbound

3. Examine roots while rootball is out of pot. If roots are fine and white in a loose mass, pot in same-size container. If roots are circled and matted, pot in next-size larger container.

4. Place plant in center of new pot. Hold plant and add soil around roots, firming as you go. Add soil to within 1/2 inch of rim.

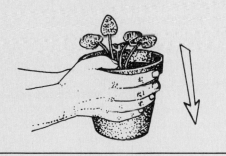

5. Firm soil by gently bumping bottom of pot on flat surface or by pressing soil with your fingers. Be sure plant is planted at correct depth—as it was in previous container.

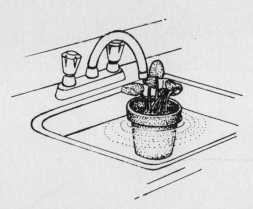

6. Place pot in a pan or sink filled with lukewarm water. Leave in water until soil surface is wet. Remove pot from water and allow to drain. Place pot in water again and drain a second time.

7. Cover plant with plastic bag to increase humidity and retain moisture. Keep leaves out of contact with plastic. Place away from strong light. Remove plastic after 3 to 4 weeks. Water plant sparingly, keeping soil slightly moist.

Fluorescent lights provide plants with proper amounts of light and add a decorative touch to the home.

Light is the single most difficult condition to correctly supply African violets and other gesneriads. Growing plants using available, natural light that enters a home requires knowledge of the sun, weather and seasons, and how they affect light conditions.

Light influences the rate of growth and formation of *chlorophyll,* the green substance found in leaves and present in all growing plants. Under the stimulus of light, chlorophyll bodies called *chloroplasts* are active in the production of plant food. The food produced is mainly starch, along with some sugar from the combination of carbon dioxide and water. This process is called *photosynthesis.* Additional factors influenced by photosynthesis are leaf size, bud formation and flowering.

A number of factors affect the quality and intensity of natural light. These are day length, weather, season (equinox), time of day, direction of sun, latitude and elevation. African violets, like all plants, need light to grow. Bright light, but not strong, direct sunlight, is ideal.

Which window exposure provides the best light for your plants? First, a brief explanation of the sun and the seasons. The earth rotates around the sun each year. The 23-1/2° tilt of its axis causes unequal periods of daylight and darkness. Only around March 21, the spring solstice, and around September 21, the fall solstice, are day and night equal in length. During summer, the sun appears high in the sky and shines for a longer period than during winter. In the Northern Hemisphere the summer equinox, longest day of the year, occurs on June 21. This is also the day that the sun is most intense. December 21, the winter equinox, is the shortest day of the year, when sunlight is weakest.

When selecting a window exposure for your plants, be aware of these seasonal changes. A northeastern or northwestern exposure receiving sun in summer might not receive any sun in winter.

Southern Exposure—This exposure receives the most light. For most of the year, sunlight will be direct and strong. Generally, place African violets in this exposure *only* during midwinter. You can then move plants to east or west exposures or provide partial shade with a sheer curtain.

Northern Exposure—North provides the least light of any exposure. It is usually too dark to grow African violets, except possibly during the longest days of the year—May 21 to July 21. By using reflecting devices such as mirrors, light exposure to plants can be increased.

Eastern Exposure—This exposure provides bright light, but not the direct sunlight of the south. It is excellent for growing African violets. During winter, you can produce more flowers by moving plants to a southern exposure.

Western Exposure—This exposure is generally preferred over others. Bright light is usually present all year. As with an eastern exposure, you may want to move plants to a southern exposure during winter.

Other Factors—Keep in mind that latitude, altitude, local weather conditions and air pollution can affect exposure. You will have to experiment to determine which works best for your plants. Consider the following:

● Latitude—The farther north you live, the longer the day length in summer and the shorter the day length in winter. Despite the longer days, sunlight is not as strong as in southern latitudes. You may find that a southern exposure, particularly during fall, winter and spring, is ideal.

● Altitude—The higher your elevation, the clearer the air and the stronger the sunlight. Even a western exposure may provide too much light under these conditions.

● Local Weather—If gray, foggy days occur frequently, a shaded, southern exposure may be preferred to an eastern or western exposure. This is often the case in the Pacific Northwest.

● Air Pollution—Dirty air reduces the strength of the sun's rays. If you live in a city with air pollution, adapt accordingly. Again, southern exposure may be right for your plants except during the warmest time of year.

● Shade Trees—If you have a large tree that shades the south side of your house, summer light filtered through the leaves may be ideal. If the tree is deciduous and loses its leaves during winter, direct winter light may also be ideal.

In the United States and Canada, normal daylight hours provide sufficient light to bring African violets into bloom, provided you select the right exposure for your situation.

Light intensity decreases drastically as the distance away from a light source increases. Generally, keep African violets as close as possible to window or other light source without exposing them to strong direct light. Every week, give each plant a quarter-turn so plant growth will be uniform. Plant will grow evenly on all sides. If plants are not turned, the side closest to the sun will develop more rapidly, resulting in a lopsided plant.

GROWING AFRICAN VIOLETS UNDER ARTIFICIAL LIGHT

You can expect reasonable success if you grow African violets in natural light available through windows and skylights. However, artificial light produces more consistent results. Because the duration and intensity of light can be controlled, plants grow larger, more vigorously and bloom regularly. Using artificial light, plants can be grown in homes having less than ideal natural light. In addition, places away from bright windows—bookshelves, closets, cellars and dark corners—can serve as growing and display areas.

Plants grow more vigorously when exposed to artificial light as compared to natural light. Vigorous plant growth requires that you pay close attention to plant's water and fertilizer needs.

To understand how to use artificial light, you need to know a little about the sun and the color spectrum. You can see the color spectrum when sunlight passes through a prism. Infrared and ultralight rays are at either end of the spectrum. Between these are red, green and blue rays among others. Red rays cause flowering and elongation and expansion of various plant parts. If a plant is exposed to only red rays, plants mature rapidly but are tall and spindly. Blue rays cause foliage growth. A plant exposed to only blue rays becomes compact with rich, dark leaves but few flowers. African violets, other gesneriads and most all plants require both red and blue rays for growth.

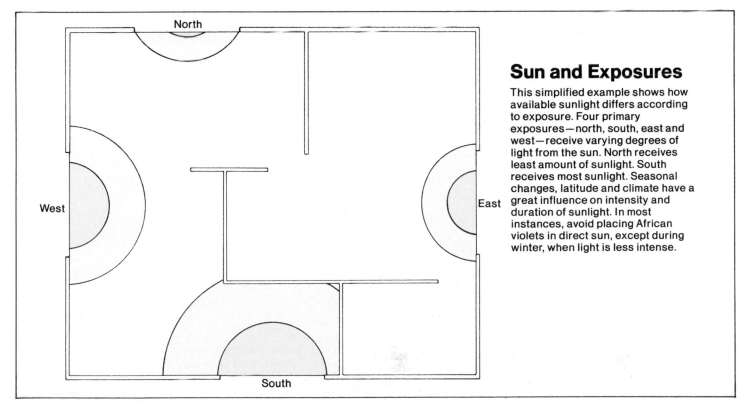

Sun and Exposures

This simplified example shows how available sunlight differs according to exposure. Four primary exposures—north, south, east and west—receive varying degrees of light from the sun. North receives least amount of sunlight. South receives most sunlight. Seasonal changes, latitude and climate have a great influence on intensity and duration of sunlight. In most instances, avoid placing African violets in direct sun, except during winter, when light is less intense.

Artificial lights for plant growth are available in two general types: *fluorescent* and *incandescent*. Fluorescent lights are the long, tube-shape lamps used most often in office buildings and stores. Incandescent lights are the regular light bulbs used in the home. There are several variations of these two types. The most common are discussed below.

Common incandescent lights do not produce the full range of light required by plants for proper growth. They generate a lot of heat—enough to burn leaves of tender plants. Exceptions exist in the form of special incandescent *plant-growth bulbs.* Some types, called *cool beams,* have a built-in reflecting device that prevents plants from becoming too hot. They also have red and blue light rays necessary for plant growth.

Fluorescent lights are preferred over incandescent light for plant growth. They are more economical, using about one-third the energy of incandescents to produce the same wattage. They last up to 20 times longer than incandescents. They emit little heat, so plant foliage is not damaged, even when placed within 6 inches of lights.

Fluorescent light tubes are available in several forms and colors. For the purposes of plant growth, you need to be familiar with these three:
• Standard cool-white (CW). This tube emits primarily blue rays of the light spectrum.
• Standard warm-white (WW) daylight. This tube emits primarily the red range of the light spectrum.
• Plant-growth and wide-spectrum tubes sold specifically for growing plants. These tubes emit both blue and red rays, and are a bit more expensive than conventional tubes. Plant-growth tubes are marketed under such trade names as Gro-Lux, Plant Gro and Agro Lite.

Standard cool-white and warm-white lamps come in two types: *preheat* and *rapid start.* Preheat tubes are cheaper and have longer life than rapid start. For plant growth, preheat tubes are satisfactory.

Fluorescent tubes are attached to fixtures by pins at both ends. For the cultivation of African violets and most other house plants, the two-pin, also called *medium bi-pin,* is the most common. Fixtures accommodating these tubes are readily available at hardware and department stores.

BASIC FLUORESCENT LIGHT
Most experts recommend a combination of cool-white and warm-white fluorescent tubes. Many growers have excellent results using one of each in a two-tube fixture, providing plants with red and blue rays. They are so successful with this arrangement they feel special plant-growth or wide-spectrum tubes are not worth the additional cost.

Other growers favor either the plant-growth or wide-spectrum tubes. These tubes were developed to *reduce* amounts of green and yellow rays of the light spectrum, colors that are not known to influence plant growth. Blue and red rays are *increased* so lights produce a slightly purplish or pink glow. These enhance the color of leaves and flowers. Green foliage looks more lush. Reds are redder, pinks appear to glow and blues and purples shimmer.

Some growers feel plants look artificial in this light. They prefer to use certain wide-spectrum tubes such as Gro-Lux Wide Spectrum, Vita-Lite and Naturescent Optima. These cast a more natural, aesthetically pleasing pink light. This is because the *far-red* of the light

Light and Plant Growth
How a plant grows in a certain exposure will tell you if light conditions are correct. Use these general symptoms as a guide to your plant's light requirements.

Too Much Light
Leaves are pale, gray and turn downward. Or leaves are yellow, hard and brittle with brown edges. Growth is compact and center of plant is bunched together. White sections of variegated leaves turn green.

Too Little Light
Plant stretches in direction of light. Leaf stems—*petioles*—become extended. Leaves are deep, rich green. Flowers, if any exist, are few in number.

spectrum is present in the coloration. African violets and other plants are more attractive when grown under these lights.

Standard, preheat fluorescent tubes last from 6,000 to 22,500 hours, depending on how often they are turned on and off. "Firing-up" of tubes reduces their life span. As tubes age, they blacken and light output diminishes. When black rings can be seen at either end of the tubes, it is time to replace them. Most growers replace tubes every 6 to 12 months to be sure plants are receiving proper light. To keep track of how long tubes have been in service, mark the ends with a grease pencil to indicate installation date.

Fluorescent tubes are sold in sizes ranging from 24 to 96 inches long and fit into standard fluorescent lamp fixtures. The most common fixture is 4 feet long, accommodating two 40-watt tubes. Most fixtures have a built-in reflector, either brushed aluminum or a flat-white painted surface. If you are purchasing a new fixture, buy a unit that has a reflector. If you have an old fixture that does not have a reflecting surface, make one with aluminum foil and install it above the tubes.

Accessories—Timers that turn lights on and off at predetermined intervals are handy items. A timer ensures that plants receive correct amounts of light every day. You don't have to worry about turning lights on or off. A timer is not necessary, but the small financial investment saves time and trouble.

Thermometers are helpful in checking temperatures around plants. Sometimes, particularly during summer, even the small amount of heat from fluorescent lights increases the soil temperature to an unhealthy level. Place the thermometer at plant level for an accurate reading. If temperatures are consistently too high—above 80F (27C)—increase air circulation with a small, electric fan. If plants are grown under lights in an enclosed area such as a cellar, closet or attic, a fan will be necessary to provide movement of stagnant air. Don't allow fan to blow directly on plants. Place it so it moves air around the room.

HOW MUCH ARTIFICIAL LIGHT?

If you use the recommended combination of cool-white and warm-white daylight fluorescent tubes, supply plants with 12 to 14 hours of light per day. Place lamps 8 to 10 inches above tops of standard African violets. Place miniature African violets about 6 inches away from the light source. Elevate miniatures on inverted pots if they are grown with standard plants under the same lighting fixture.

If you move African violets from natural to artificial light, provide plants with a period of adjustment. The first week, place plants under artificial lights for 8 hours a day. The next week, place them under lights for 10 hours a day. Each week, extend the lighting period by 2 hours a day until you reach the recommended 12 to 14 hours.

Light from fluorescents is most intense in the middle of the tube. If you look at a fluorescent light, you can see the difference in intensity. African violets with dark-green foliage and dark blooms usually absorb more light. Place these plants under the middle portion of tubes where light is strongest. Plants with light-green leaves and white or pink flowers require and absorb less light. Place these plants under the ends of tubes, where light is weaker. See illustration below.

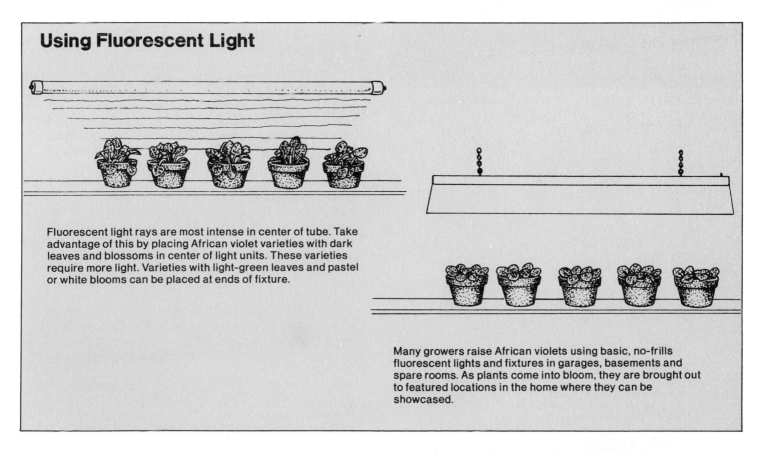

Using Fluorescent Light

Fluorescent light rays are most intense in center of tube. Take advantage of this by placing African violet varieties with dark leaves and blossoms in center of light units. These varieties require more light. Varieties with light-green leaves and pastel or white blooms can be placed at ends of fixture.

Many growers raise African violets using basic, no-frills fluorescent lights and fixtures in garages, basements and spare rooms. As plants come into bloom, they are brought out to featured locations in the home where they can be showcased.

African violets and other gesneriads require regular amounts of water to grow properly and produce flowers. No rules exist as to how often and how much to water individual plants. Soil should be kept moist but never soggy. Soil containing a large proportion of moisture-retaining material, such as horticultural vermiculite, perlite or sphagnum moss, requires water less frequently than soil that drains freely.

Overwatering is the most common cause of failure of African violets. Plants have been known to survive waterlogged conditions, but they do not bloom or grow satisfactorily. If given the choice, it is better to underwater than to overwater.

WHEN TO WATER

Frequency of watering and amount differ with the plant and situation. Size and type of pot have a great effect. Clay pots are porous, so evaporation of moisture is more rapid than with plastic pots. Plants in clay pots require water more frequently. Small pots hold less water, so require more attention to watering than large pots.

During warm, summer months, water evaporates faster than during cool months. Vigorous-growing plants use more water than slow-growing plants. Keep this in mind as plants go through seasonal growth fluctuations. For example, plants grow fast in spring and slow down in winter.

The best way to determine water need is to check the potting soil with your fingers. When top 1/2 inch of soil is dry to the touch, it is time to water. To maintain health and growth, water before plants show signs of needing water—lackluster leaf color, droopy appearance. Avoid this stress and plants will produce more flowers.

WATERING METHODS

There is a misconception about water damaging the leaves of African violets. As long as water is not cold and wet leaves are not exposed to direct sunlight, damage should not result. Cold water on leaves can cause brown spots to develop. Apply water that is room temperature. A simple way to do this is to draw a jug of water the night before you water plants. If leaves do get wet, don't expose plants to direct sunlight. Sun shining through water will burn leaves.

Top Watering—Use a watering can that has a long spout or a poultry baster to apply water under leaves. This way water does not get on the foliage and in the crown. This method also helps avoid splashing soil on the leaves.

When watering plants from the top, place a saucer or tray under pot to catch excess water. Empty water after it has drained through soil so pot won't be left "standing" in water. Problems can develop if roots are waterlogged.

Bottom Watering—Fill saucer or tray beneath pot with water. Water is drawn up into soil. After about two hours, pour off excess water from saucer or tray. Check top of soil in pot for moisture.

Wick watering is simple, easy-care way to water plants.

Wick Watering—Many growers favor a wick-watering method. Watering this way is especially useful if plants must be left unattended for extended periods. Wick watering works in the same manner as an old-fashion oil lamp. Water is absorbed by an absorbent material. It can be an oil-lamp wick, cotton string or nylon stocking cut into strips. Wick is placed in a reservoir of water located beneath or adjacent to plant pot. Water is drawn from the reservoir up the wick and into the pot, moistening the soil.

Capillary Matting—These systems are commonly used by African violet hobbyists. The way the matting works is simple. Pots are placed on wet mats designed to retain moisture. Water is absorbed by capillary action from mat into pot through the drainage holes. This system is advantageous if you have a large collection of plants, because less time is required than for other methods. In addition to watering plants almost automatically, mats increase humidity.

Commercial capillary matting is a ruglike material made from synthetic fibers. Mats are sold under the names of Vattex P, Water Mat and Thermalem. They are available at garden centers or greenhouse-supply companies. You can make your own mats out of synthetic blankets, fake fur or fluffy polyester material. Natural fibers are not recommended because they become moldy and stagnant. The material should be loosely woven and able to hold water.

Water pots and place on dampened mats. Use pots that have drain holes in the pot bottom and not on the sides so water can be absorbed. The pot should sink down into it, so there is good contact between base of pot and matting. Mats can be kept constantly damp or allowed to dry out before watering again.

A disadvantage of capillary mats is they encourage algae and insect growth. Some pests, such as nematodes and soil mealy bugs, can travel through the water to infest plants. Check mats every two months. If problems occur, soak mats in a mild solution of detergent and household chlorine bleach. Rinse mats with water and replace under pots. Sprinkle systemic granular insecticide over the mat.

ALTERNATE METHODS

It is a good practice to switch between top and bottom watering. If you bottom water and feed plants with water-soluble fertilizer at the same time, fertilizer salts accumulate on top of soil. These salts also form a crust on the pot's top rim, especially with clay pots. When the leaf *petiole*—the leaf stem—comes in contact with the salts, it can rot. Avoid this by supplying regular liquid feeding by top watering. Switch to bottom watering until it is time to feed again. If fertilizer salts do form, water thoroughly from the top by flushing the container soil. See page 27.

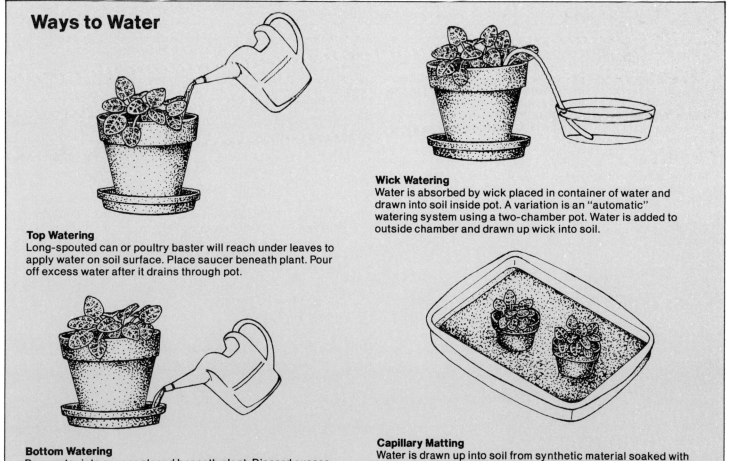

Ways to Water

Top Watering
Long-spouted can or poultry baster will reach under leaves to apply water on soil surface. Place saucer beneath plant. Pour off excess water after it drains through pot.

Bottom Watering
Pour water into saucer placed beneath plant. Discard excess after water has been absorbed by plant and soil mix.

Wick Watering
Water is absorbed by wick placed in container of water and drawn into soil inside pot. A variation is an "automatic" watering system using a two-chamber pot. Water is added to outside chamber and drawn up wick into soil.

Capillary Matting
Water is drawn up into soil from synthetic material soaked with water. Be sure pots have drain holes in bottom of pot and make good contact with mat.

Making a Wick-Watering System

Wick pots designed for use with African violets are available at garden centers and from mail-order sources. It is easy to make a system from ordinary household items. Plastic butter tubs or plastic food-storage containers make excellent water reservoirs. Translucent container is best so you can see when water is low.

1. Make wick from absorbent material such as rope, strips of nylon stocking or oil-lamp wick. Wick should reach from pot to water reservoir. Unravel several inches at one end and soak in water.
2. Place unraveled end of wick down through drainage hole of pot. Evenly spread unraveled end over inside of pot bottom and press down to hold in place.
3. Cover wick in bottom of pot with about 1/2 inch of moistened soil mix. Be sure wick remains in place.

Option:

4. Fill pot with more soil mix and pot plant. Water from top until water drips from wick extending beneath pot.
5. Fill water reservoir with room-temperature water. Place wick in water reservoir, but keep base of pot out of water. One way to do this is to place potted plant on inverted pot.
Option: Use a water reservoir that has a lid. Make a hole in lid so wick can be submerged in water and place plant on top of reservoir. See photo, page 20.

When You Go Away

If you will be absent from home for an extended period, take some precautions to ensure the health of your plants. Locate plants where they will receive bright light but no direct sun. Moisten soil with water, but do not saturate. Remove leaves, petioles and blossoms that are drooping or brown. Remove flower buds that will bloom during your absence. Inspect plants for insects and diseases. Isolate infected plants.

Any of the methods shown here should keep plants healthy and watered for about two weeks. If you wick-water African violets, use a large water reservoir. A half-gallon container should supply plants with water for a month or longer.

Lay capillary mat in sink and allow faucet to drip slowly onto it. Place pots on top of mat.

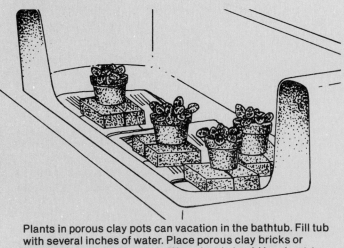

Plants in porous clay pots can vacation in the bathtub. Fill tub with several inches of water. Place porous clay bricks or stacks of newspapers in tub. Water level should be about 1 inch below level of bricks and papers. Set pots on top. Water is absorbed through bottom of pots.

Group plants and cover with sheet of clear plastic. Or cover individual plants with plastic wrap. Place sticks in soil around plants to form tent so plastic will not be in contact with foliage.

Trays filled with water increase humidity around plants as water evaporates. Marbles keep bottom of pot above water level and add a bright splash of color.

African violets and other gesneriads thrive in temperatures that are comfortable for you. Daytime temperatures between 72F and 75F (22C to 24C), and nighttime temperatures between 67F and 70F (20C to 21C) are ideal.

All gesneriads can adapt to a wide range of temperatures. They will endure nighttime temperatures of 45F to 50F (7C to 10C) if daytime temperatures climb to around 70F (21C). If temperature changes are *gradual*, plants usually survive. *Sudden* temperature changes can injure or kill plants. If temperatures fall below 60F (16C), growth slows, bloom is sparse and foliage usually sustains minor damage. Warm summer temperatures adversely affect plant growth. If temperatures are consistently above 85F (30C), plants will be spindly, and most blossoms will drop off before reaching mature size.

As a rule, it is better if temperatures are cool rather than hot. This is because African violets are more naturally adapted to cool temperatures. Even if temperatures occasionally reach 80F to 90F (27C to 32C), plants have the ability to survive these extreme conditions.

Most homes have a wide range of temperature and humidity levels. These levels change with the seasons. Heaters, air conditioners and doorways create hot spots, cold spots and drafts. During winter, glass in windows can become cold. Exposure can damage plants if they come in contact with glass or are close to glass. If plants cannot be moved, place cardboard, newspaper or other materials for insulation between plants and windows. Close shades or draperies at night for additional protection. Identifying locations in your home can help avoid problems with temperature, humidity and ventilation.

HUMIDITY

In their natural habitat—Tanzania, Africa—African violets grow in an atmosphere containing 70% to 80% humidity. African violets and their relatives can thrive at lower levels—40% to 60% humidity. Humidity levels of 40% or more are not difficult to provide in a home environment. The effort is worth it. Plants grown in high humidity produce larger and more abundant blooms. They require less light and are able to absorb nutrients easier if humidity is closer to natural conditions.

In most areas of North America, except for the dry, southwestern United States, humidity levels average between 50% and 60% during the non-heating season. This is satisfactory for all gesneriads. During the winter heating months, humidity levels often drop to 25% or below. This is unhealthy for your plants, and for yourself.

A *hygrometer* can be used to measure humidity. These are sometimes available at horticultural suppliers, hardware stores or through mail-order sources. During the winter heating months, you should *always* plan on raising the humidity substantially.

RAISING HUMIDITY

There are several ways to raise humidity.

Capillary mats are devices that are saturated with water to supply plants with moisture and fertilizer. As the water in the mats evaporates, the humidity increases around plants. See page 21.

Humidity trays can be placed under pots. These are shallow, rectangular trays filled with pebbles. Marbles can also be used for a colorful effect. Trays are filled with water and pots are placed on pebbles or marbles above water level. *Be sure bottom of pot is not in contact with water.* If it stays in contact, soil in pots can become waterlogged, forcing out air. This will injure or kill roots. Keep water level below surface of pebbles, or set plants on inverted flower pots.

Group plants together, but not too closely or air circulation will be decreased. As plants *transpire,* draw in carbon dioxide and release oxygen and moisture, humidity is increased.

Misting with fogger-sprayers or other items raises humidity. Mist in the vicinity of plants, not directly on foliage. Do not mist plants with cold water. Use room-temperature water. Mist plants when they are out of direct sunlight.

Fill bottles or jars with water and place among plants. Leave them open so water can evaporate to increase humidity.

Electric humidifiers are inexpensive and require little energy to operate. Place them about 10 feet from plants and run them day or night.

In some regions, the humidity may be so low it can't be raised for any length of time by any of the preceding methods. The desert region of the Southwest is an example. It may be better to grow plants in terrariums, which maintain high levels of humidity. See page 48 for additional information.

Newly transplanted African violets grow best when humidity is high. Enclose plants in clear plastic bags until they are established. Keep foliage out of contact with plastic by forming a wire support over plant.

Ways to Increase Humidity

African violets and most other house plants benefit from high humidity. It is not too difficult to raise humidity in vicinity of plants. It is also beneficial to provide good air circulation, which helps prevent diseases.

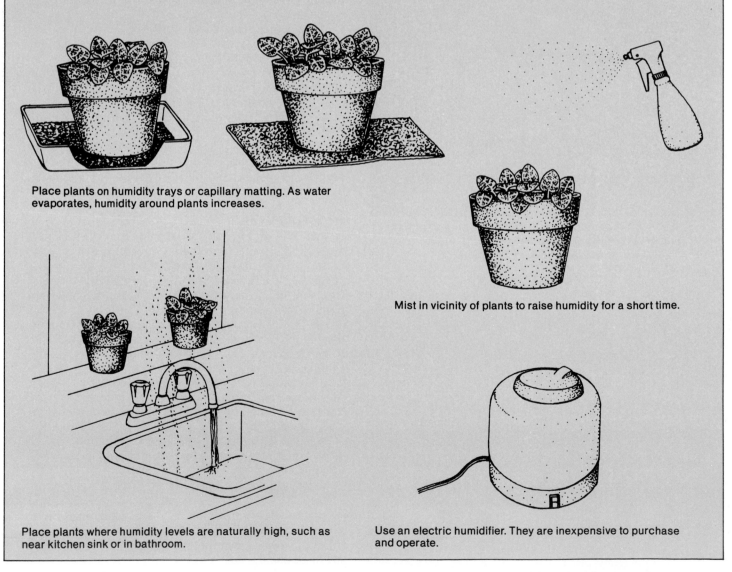

Place plants on humidity trays or capillary matting. As water evaporates, humidity around plants increases.

Mist in vicinity of plants to raise humidity for a short time.

Place plants where humidity levels are naturally high, such as near kitchen sink or in bathroom.

Use an electric humidifier. They are inexpensive to purchase and operate.

VENTILATION

African violets and other gesneriads require indirect air circulation for good health but do not do well in drafts. Never let air or breezes blow directly on them. Without ventilation, mildew and other diseases may occur. Be sure there is air circulation within the plant room and around plants. Space plants about 6 inches apart.

During warm, summer months, air circulation is adequate if a window near plants is kept open. Even so, it is a good idea to open doors and allow air to circulate a couple of times each day—once in the morning and again in midafternoon. Circulation of air will also help lower temperatures. Operating a small electric fan near plants provides air circulation, but don't allow breeze to blow directly on plants. In regions experiencing hot summers, the air conditioning you provide for your own comfort will usually accommodate the plants as well.

During winter months the usual coming and going of people in and out of a house provides enough circulation. If this is not the case, close the door to the room where plants are located and open a window in a nearby room for a short time. Then close the window, allow the air to warm a bit, and open the door of your plant room. The new but warm outside air will circulate into the room to the benefit of your plants.

Ventilation in cellars, attics, closets or small windowless rooms is usually poor. Provide air circulation by installing small fans nearby.

A special problem may occur if you cook or heat with gas. A small, slow leak, not noticeable or harmful to humans, may affect plants. Flower buds may turn black and drop, and foliage may yellow. For the health of your plants and your own health, have the gas company inspect for leaks if you think your stove or waterheater is malfunctioning. This is usually done free of charge.

Trouble Spots in the Home

Certain locations in your home may not be best for plant growth, or can injure or kill plants. Avoid placing plants where they are exposed to drafts, such as near doors and windows that do not fit snugly. Refrigerators, dishwashers and heating vents produce excessive heat. Gas leaks from stoves and waterheaters can kill plants.

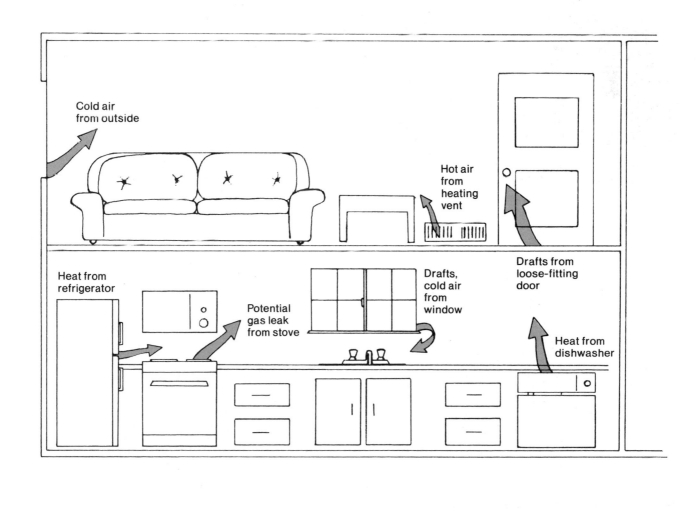

Cold air from outside

Hot air from heating vent

Drafts from loose-fitting door

Heat from refrigerator

Potential gas leak from stove

Drafts, cold air from window

Heat from dishwasher

Fertilizers are available in two basic types: chemical, *inorganic fertilizer,* left, and *organic fertilizer,* such as fish emulsion, right.

African violets and other gesneriads require certain nutrients for growth. Type of fertilizer and when and how much to feed varies according to plant condition, soil mixture, moisture, humidity and other factors. You will probably have to experiment with different fertilizers and methods to determine the best system and schedule for your plants.

Overfertilizing plants is a common mistake made by many growers. If African violets receive large, frequent doses, salts collect in the soil and on pot rim, causing root, crown and stem rot. Plants showing signs of nutrient deficiency have dull foliage and blooms lack a sharp luster. But these are more likely to be symptoms of other problems, such as an infestation of aphids or other pest. See Pests and Diseases, page 28, to determine if something else is bothering plants before adding more fertilizer.

ESSENTIAL NUTRIENTS

All plants require 13 essential elements for healthy growth. Six are major elements: nitrogen, phosphorus, potassium, calcium, magnesium and sulfur. These nutrients are available in most commercial fertilizers. The amounts of nitrogen, phosphorus and potassium are indicated by numbers on the product label. These represent percentages of the nutrients contained in the product. African violets and other gesneriads require a balanced formula. A ratio such as 20-20-20 is common. This means the formula will contain 20% nitrogen, 20% phosphorus and 20% potassium.

The remaining seven minor elements are called *trace elements.* They include boron, chlorine, copper, iron, manganese, molybdenum and zinc. With rare exceptions, these are present in commercial African violet soil mixes.

TYPES OF FERTILIZERS

A wide range of packaged, commercial African violet fertilizers is available. They can be used for other gesneriads. These include *chemical, inorganic fertilizers,* and *natural, organic fertilizers.*

Natural, Organic Fertilizers—These are derived from living organisms instead of chemical salts. Popular kinds include bone meal, blood meal, fish emulsion and animal manure products. Fish emulsion is the most popular. Organic fertilizers are satisfactory for part of the nutrient needs of African violets, but they do not provide all essential elements. Using these products exclusively may result in plants having deficiencies of nitrogen, phosphorus and potassium.

Chemical, Inorganic Fertilizers—These are manufactured from chemical salts and available in a number of forms. Powders—termed *water soluble*—are mixed in water. Fertilizers are given to plants with watering. As a guide, apply water-soluble fertilizers at two-thirds the amount recommended by the manufacturer. For example, if the product label recommends mixing 1 teaspoon fertilizer with 1 gallon water, use 2/3 teaspoon fertilizer. Most manufacturers recommend fertilizing at specific intervals, such as once a month or once every eight weeks.

Concentrated liquid fertilizers are diluted with water. They too are given to plants with watering. Experienced African violet growers usually fertilize with a *weak* solution of liquid fertilizer each time plants are watered. If instructions call for 1 level teaspoon of food per gallon of water, use one-fourth of that amount per gallon to make a weak solution.

Time-release capsules are mixed into the soil. Moisture breaks down the capsule wall and nutrients are released over a period of weeks or months, depending on the product. If plants are watered from the top, sprinkle capsules on the soil surface. Time-release fertilizer does not last indefinitely. You'll have to supplement with other fertilizers such as liquid or granular forms. If plants are watered from the bottom or wick watered, mix capsules thoroughly in soil when plants are potted.

Foliar feeding—spraying leaves with a nutrient solution—is generally not recommended. Benefits to plants are inconclusive. Better results are obtained when plant roots absorb nutrients and distribute them to the plant.

A better balance of nutrients can be supplied by alternating use of organic and inorganic fertilizers. It is also a good idea to use different ratios of inorganic fertilizers. Providing your plants with a more balanced diet will result in more flowers.

Salts from chemical fertilizers build up in the soil, on the soil surface and along the top rim of the plant's container. Each time you water plants with a liquid fertilizer solution, add enough so it seeps out of the pot bottom. This lets you know that nutrients are distributed throughout the soil.

LEACH SOIL SALTS
Once a month, flush soil thoroughly with water. This *leaches* the soil of fertilizer salts—washes them out and away from plant roots. Slowly pour an amount of water equal to five times the pot volume through the soil. If you don't leach the soil, foliage may develop stem rot where the stem comes into contact with salts on the soil surface and pot rim. In addition, build up of salts in the root zone can damage sensitive roots.

FERTILIZER TIPS
Under certain conditions plants should not be fertilized or fertilizer amounts should be reduced.

• After a plant has bloomed profusely, don't fertilize for at least a week. This is particularly important with large-flowering varieties, such as some of the Optimara and Ballet strains.

• During periods of low sunlight, such as overcast winter days, plants do not grow vigorously. Reduce or eliminate fertilizer applications during periods of slow growth.

• Most African violets require little, if any, fertilizer right after potting or propagating. The new soil usually has enough nutrients to supply plant needs. Wait a month before fertilizing.

• If plant looks unhealthy, stop fertilizing. In most cases, the problem is caused by factors other than lack of fertilizer. If you continue to fertilize, problems could become more severe. Check Pests and Diseases, page 28, for a guide to plant problems.

• If plants are fertilized every four to eight weeks, do not pour dry fertilizer or a liquid nutrient solution on dry soil. Wet soil with plain water and then apply fertilizer.

• If plants are in porous clay pots, cover rims with aluminum foil or dip rims in melted paraffin. This prevents fertilizer salts from accumulating on the pot rim.

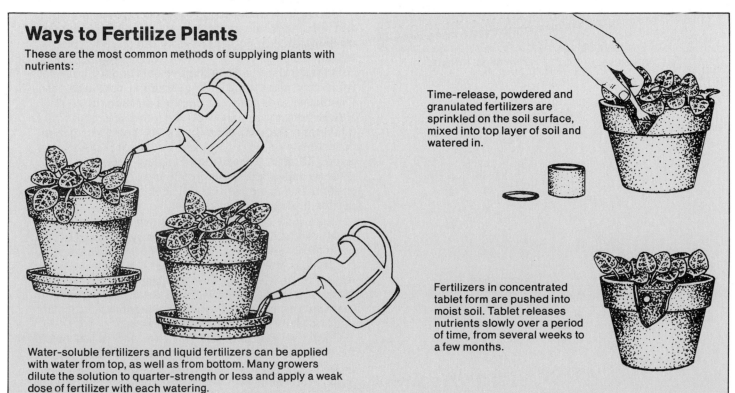

Ways to Fertilize Plants
These are the most common methods of supplying plants with nutrients:

Time-release, powdered and granulated fertilizers are sprinkled on the soil surface, mixed into top layer of soil and watered in.

Fertilizers in concentrated tablet form are pushed into moist soil. Tablet releases nutrients slowly over a period of time, from several weeks to a few months.

Water-soluble fertilizers and liquid fertilizers can be applied with water from top, as well as from bottom. Many growers dilute the solution to quarter-strength or less and apply a weak dose of fertilizer with each watering.

Check your plants every few days to avoid an infestation such as this.

Pests and diseases occasionally infest house plants, and African violets are no exception. If you follow the prevention guidelines listed in this section, you will probably avoid serious problems with pests and diseases. Providing good growing conditions and observing precautions will produce plants with healthy growth and glorious bloom and beauty.

The following pages describe some of the most common insects and diseases known to bother African violets and other gesneriads. In all cases, follow the manufacturer's recommendations and cautions for mixing and applying products.

SANITATION

Prevention is a key word when it comes to caring for African violets. Eliminating problems before they become established is the best treatment of pests and diseases. Follow the guidelines listed below for healthy plants.

An Ounce of Prevention—When you bring new plants home, it's tempting to put them on the shelf or windowsill along with your existing collection. But doing this invites trouble. It is best to quarantine new plants. Often, pests or diseases are introduced to a healthy collection of plants by a new, infected plant. For one month, keep new plants at least 18 inches away from your established collection. If possible, keep new plants in a separate room.

After handling new plants, wash your hands thoroughly with hot, soapy water, before you work with established collections. Avoid having your clothing come in contact with new plants. Pests and diseases can spread this way.

During the quarantine period, use separate watering and feeding implements for new plants. Or sterilize implements with boiling water before tending your established plants.

Do not brush leaves to remove dust and soil particles from new plants until the quarantine period is past. Dusting spreads pests and diseases through the air.

If plants show no signs of pests or diseases after the quarantine period, add them to your permanent collection.

Keep Plants Clean—Immediately remove dead flowers, stalks, leaves and decaying vegetative matter as soon as you notice them. Check plants every other day for any signs of decaying matter.

Clean dust from foliage by showering plants with tepid, room-temperature water. It may be necessary to wash plants once a week, once a month or twice a year, depending on conditions. The bathtub is a good place to give plants a shower. Allow foliage to dry away from direct sunlight and drafts, then return to permanent location. Inspect plants for insects and diseases. Isolate infested plants from groupings and treat.

Check soil surface and pot rims for salt deposits from fertilizers. Use a damp cloth to remove salts from pot rim. *Leach* salts from soil by washing them out and away from plant roots. About once a month, pour a large amount of water through the soil. As a guide, pour an amount equal to five times the volume of the pot.

Precautions When Potting—Use pasteurized soil and sterilized pots and saucers when potting plants. Commercial soil mixes are usually labeled as being sterilized or pasteurized. If you prepare your own soil mix, sterilize or pasteurize as described on page 12.

Wash and soak all pots, tubs and saucers before potting. Use a disinfecting solution of 1 quart hot, soapy water to 1 cup household bleach. Soak containers for at least 10 minutes. Afterward, rinse in warm water to remove bleach and soap.

Cut Flowers—Keep cut flowers away from your plant collections. Flowers sometimes carry diseases that can be transmitted to your African violets.

SAFETY PRECAUTIONS WHEN USING CHEMICALS

- Follow instructions on the package to the letter. Do not add additional chemicals for "good measure."
- Mix only enough spray for one application. Discard leftover chemical solutions in a safe place. Do not save chemical sprays for a future application.
- When spraying, wear a protective mask or place a wet towel over nose and mouth.
- Wear a long-sleeved shirt and gloves while spraying to protect the skin. Wash all exposed skin areas thoroughly with hot, soapy water after each spraying.
- While spraying, stir mixture or shake sprayer frequently to keep chemicals from settling.
- Use the right spray for the pest or disease you wish to control.
- Never use any container or instruments used to mix or store chemicals for another purpose. Apply a skull and crossbones sticker on bottles and implements used to mix chemical sprays.
- Store all chemicals and mixing implements in a safe place out of reach of children and pets.
- Dispose of all unused and empty chemical bottles in a safe place.

Preventing Problems

Maintaining a clean growing environment and providing regular care prevents infection of most pests and diseases. Follow these precautions.

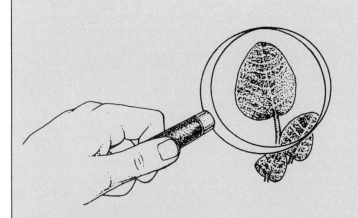

Isolate all new plants for at least one month before adding them to your collection. Keep new plants about 18 inches away from established plants. Use separate set of watering implements to prevent spread of pests or diseases.

Remove flowers, stems and leaves as soon as they are past prime.

Inspect plants frequently, especially undersides of leaves. Use a magnifying glass to check for tiny pests such as spider mites.

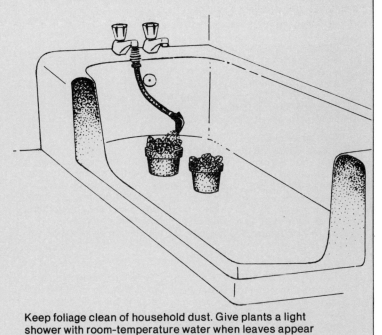

Keep foliage clean of household dust. Give plants a light shower with room-temperature water when leaves appear dusty.

Insect Pests

Aphids or Plant Lice
Winged and wingless forms in green, red, pink, black or brown. Easy to spot on plants. They measure 1/16 to 1/8 inch long. Bodies are rounded and pear shape, with long legs and antennae. Aphids cluster around new, growing tips and the undersides of leaves, sucking juices. Foliage and new shoots turn pale, curl up and die. Secretions of *honeydew,* a glossy, sticky substance, are evident on leaves. This secretion may host *sooty mold,* a black fungus.

Treatment: Isolate plants. If infestation is light, remove insects with fingers or dab them with cotton swabs soaked in rubbing alcohol. Wash leaves with water after alcohol treatment. Or hold plants upside down in warm, soapy water for about two minutes, then rinse with clean water. Water plant before immersing and soil will not fall out. To treat a heavy infestation, spray plant with a product containing malathion or Orthene. Repeat treatment every 5 to 7 days until aphids are gone. Or drench pot with a solution containing dimethoate. Follow directions on label. To be certain you are rid of infestation, repeat drench after 7 days. As a preventive, drench plants every 6 months or spray once a month with all-purpose house and garden insect spray such as Raid House and Garden Bug Killer.

Blackflies
Blackflies swarm around plants. Bodies are 1/16 inch long. Insects do little physical damage to plants, but can become a nuisance. If infestation is heavy, root damage may result. Blackfly larvae feed on the roots of African violet plants.

Treatment: Spray with Orthene or all-purpose house and garden insect spray. If infestation persists, drench soil with a solution of dimethoate to kill blackfly larvae and eggs.

Leaf Mealy Bug
Mealy bugs look like white puffs of cotton clustered under leaves, on ends of shaded leaves, in leaf axils, in crotches of stems and deep in the crown. They are 1/4 inch long and coated with a white, powdery wax. They suck juices from plants, stunting growth. Plant may die if insects are not eliminated.

Treatment: Isolate plant. For minor infestation, dip cotton swab in alcohol and apply to insects and to spot on plant where insects were located. After alcohol treatment, wash leaves with water. Repeat treatment every 2 or 3 days until all insects have been destroyed. For serious infestations, drench or spray plant and soil with dimethoate solution. Or spray plants with a solution of malathion or Orthene. For prevention, drench soil once a month with dimethoate solution or spray with an all-purpose house and garden insect spray.

Mites
Mites are not insects, rather, they are members of the spider family. Three kinds are common house-plant pests: cyclamen mites, broad mites and red spider mites. All are invisible to the naked eye. A strong magnifying glass or microscope must be used to see them. Each mite produces different symptoms. How pests infest plant and treatment are same for all three.

Cyclamen Mite
These spiderlike pests are less than 1/100 inch long. Eggs are oval and pearl-white. White in larva stage and white to brown or amber as adults. They live in new growth in center of plants. They also live on young, tender leaves, stem ends, buds and flowers. Leaves twist and curl, turn brittle, or dusty gray. Plant growth is stunted. Excessive hairs form near the center of the plant. Flower buds may be deformed and blotched. Left untreated, center of plant may die, which usually kills the entire plant.

Broad Mite
Tiny insects about 1/150 inch long. Slightly broader and more active than cyclamen mites. Symptoms similar to infestation of cyclamen mite, except broad mites feed on lower area of leaves. This causes infected leaves to curl downward rather than upward.

Red Spider Mite
These spiderlike pests are microscopic. Oval, with greenish, yellowish or reddish bodies. They attack undersides of leaves, spinning fine, silvery or white webs that cover other parts of the plant. Yellow or brown speckles can be seen on upper surface of leaves. Plant color appears dull and sick. Webs may be visible on underside of leaves. A severe infestation can cause plants to die.

Treatment: Applies to all three mites. Isolate plant immediately. Spray plant every 5 to 7 days with dicofol until plant recovers and pests cannot be seen. As a preventive, drench plants every 6 months or spray with dicofol. If infestation is severe, discard plant. Wash hands thoroughly with hot, soapy water before handling other plants.

Root Nematodes
A common pest of gesneriads. Worms are microscopic and round. They suck juice from plants. Beadlike lumps can sometimes be seen on main roots of plant. Plants wilt, turn sickly yellow. Vigor is poor. Crown rot, described on page 32, may infect plants. In addition to attacking roots in soil, root nematodes can travel over wet surfaces and infest other plants. This is particularly a problem if plants are watered by a common method such as capillary matting. They can also travel from the potting bench to other plants.

Treatment: Discard badly infested plants. Isolate infested plants that can be revived. Drench plant with a solution of dimethoate. Drench plants again in 7 days, then again 7 days later. If plant still does not recover and is worth saving, take leaf cuttings that are not in contact with soil. Use these to propagate new plants that will not have root nematodes. Wash hands thoroughly after handling to avoid infesting healthy plants. Place saucers under individual plants to prevent spreading of nematodes.

Scale Insects
Small, oval, round or oyster shell-shape insects from 1/16 to 3/8 inches in diameter. Shell-like covering serves as a protective shelter for insect. Colors range from white to black. Most are brownish or gray. Scale can be present in unsterilized soil or pots. Scale suck juices from plants. They secrete *honeydew,* a sticky substance, that serves as host to a black fungus called *sooty mold.* Growth of plant is poor and stunted. If infestation is not stopped, plant will die.

Treatment: Isolate plant. Dip or spray with a malathion or Orthene solution. Follow manufacturer's recommendations on product label. Treat every 5 to 7 days until scale cannot be seen. Wash hands thoroughly with hot, soapy water after handling plants with scale to avoid infecting healthy plants. As a preventive measure, spray plants once a month with all-purpose house and garden insect spray.

Soil Mealy Bug
Also called *Pritchard mealy bug.* Creamy white insects, 1/16 inch long. They resemble grains of rice. Bugs can move from pot to pot if plants are watered by common watering without saucers. Although they do not spread easily, they are able to travel over wet surfaces. Unsterilized soil is also a source of infestation. Bugs attack feeder roots—tiny, white roots in upper layer of soil. Look for bugs on *new* root growth. Plant suffering from infestation looks wilted and has poor vigor. Crown rot eventually infects plants.

Treatment: Isolate plant. Spray plant every 10 days with malathion or Orthene solution. To ensure elimination of pests, spray every 7 to 10 days for 2 months. To prevent infestations, spray every 6 months.

Springtails
Threadlike, 1/5-inch-long insects. They jump in the same manner as fleas. They may live on soil surface or in saucers beneath pot. Springtails can be present in unsterilized soil used in potting. Usually seen in saucers immediately after watering. They do not harm foliage, but severe infestations can harm plant roots.

Treatment: Drench pot and saucers in solution of 1 cup household bleach per quart of hot, soapy water. To prevent infestation, pasteurize soil, pots and saucers. See page 12.

Thrips

Tiny, threadlike insects. Pale yellow when young, tan when adult. They jump and crawl when disturbed. Sucking mouths do the damage. Use magnifying glass to inspect for infestation. Symptoms are white spots on leaves with blotches and brown areas at edges. Occasionally, red specks that turn black appear. Flowers are smaller than usual, and may turn brown rapidly or drop off. Thrips pollinate flowers. Pollen spills out of stamens on flower petals. Pollen is usually visible on dark blooms.

Treatment: Isolate plant. Use a cotton swab soaked in rubbing alcohol to kill insects on stems, leaves, buds and blossoms. Wash leaves with water after alcohol treatment. Or hold plant upside down in warm, soapy water and rinse in clean water. Water plant beforehand and soil won't fall out. For heavy infestation, immerse plant in malathion solution, or spray with malathion solution. Treat with malathion every 5 to 7 days until thrips are gone. Spray soil surface with malathion or Orthene solution to kill *nymphs*—thrips at premature stage of growth. Remove all flowers and buds of infested plant. This is where thrips appear first. As a preventive measure, drench pot every 6 months with malathion solution, or spray plant once a month with all-purpose house and garden insect spray. Insect pest strips—chemically soaked materials available in hardware stores—can also be used as preventives.

Whiteflies

Tiny, white flies can be seen on plants. They suck plant juices. If leaves of infested plants are touched, whiteflies will fly from leaves. If infestation is severe, flies appear as a small, white cloud emerging from plant. Infested leaves turn pale green, change to yellow, then die and drop off plant. Whiteflies also secrete a sticky substance, called *honeydew,* that serves as host for *sooty mold,* a black fungus.

Treatment: Isolate plant. Dip or spray with malathion or Orthene solution. Follow manufacturer's instructions on product label. Repeat treatment every 5 to 7 days until flies are gone. Insect pest strips also help control.

After handling, wash hands with hot, soapy water to avoid infecting healthy plants. As a preventive measure, spray once a month with all-purpose house and garden insect spray.

Insect Pests

Mealy bug

Scale

Aphid

Thrips

Red spider mite

Cyclamen mite

Whitefly

Diseases and Cultural Problems

Botrytis Blight or Gray Mold Blight
Mold thrives in conditions of high humidity and poor air circulation. Gray mold first appears on buds and blooms, causing them to turn brown and mushy. Unchecked, leaves and stems turn brownish black and rot.
Treatment: Isolate infested plant. Immediately remove diseased and dead flowers and leaves. Space plants at least 1 foot apart to increase air circulation. Spray plant with benomyl according to manufacturer's instructions. Treat for mites, which are carriers of botrytis blight spores. See Mites, page 30.

Crown Rot
Affects roots of African violets. Caused by too much moisture in soil. Soggy, heavy soil is the best host to crown rot organisms. Overwatering can also cause this problem. Plants wilt, sometimes gradually, sometimes rapidly, as roots die. Center of plant turns brown. Plant hairs are covered with weblike substance and center leaves rot.
Treatment: Isolate plant. If severely infected, discard plant. If it looks as if plant can be saved, repot it. Remove plant from pot and gently shake off all soil from roots. Trim dead roots or soft stems to healthy growth. Dust cuts with sulfur, ferbam or captan powder. Pot in sterilized soil. Add a fungicide such as benomyl to soil. Do not overwater repotted plants. Use coarse, porous, well-draining soil. Water plants from below, or water under leaves, keeping water away from plant crown.

Green Slime
This condition is generally caused by too much moisture and lack of air circulation. It is not a serious problem but can be unattractive.
Treatment: Simply wipe pots clean when slime is evident. Pay close attention to watering. Be sure there is enough space between plants for circulation of air. In severe instances, use a small electric fan to move air in growing area. Don't allow fan to blow directly on plants.

Petiole Rot
This is not a disease. Petiole rot is caused when leaf and leaf stalk come in contact with fertilizer salts. Leaf stalks become mushy and droop at the point of contact on rim of pot or tub. An orange or rust-color lesion may develop at the point of contact. Do not confuse this discoloration with natural decline of older leaves, where leaves slowly turn yellow, wither and die. Leaves suffering from petiole rot are green when afflicted.
Treatment: Cut back afflicted leaves to healthy growth. Remove accumulated salts in soil by watering soil three times in one hour. Before watering, break up soil surface with fork. Or remove plant from pot and repot in sterilized pot. Water with distilled water.

Overfertilization is a primary cause of fertilizer salts accumulating in soil and on pot rims. Be sure plants need fertilizer before applying it. Also use distilled water and water plant from top. Plastic or glazed clay pots are not porous so do not accumulate salts as much as clay pots. If porous clay pots are used, cover rims with aluminum foil or dip rims in melted paraffin. Do not fertilize until your plant regains its health.

Powdery Mildew
White, powdery fungus. Airborne spores become active and infest plants. Conditions of high humidity, poor ventilation and sudden temperature changes promote powdery mildew. Fungus is seen on blossoms and flower stems. Flowers become small, deformed and drop early. In severe cases, round, white spots appear on leaves.
Treatment: Isolate plant. Spray with solution of benomyl. Follow manufacturer's instructions on product label. Lightly dust plants once a week with product that contains folpet, or dust with powdered sulfur. To prevent powdery mildew, provide good air circulation by installing a small fan near plants.

Ring Spot
Yellow, ring-shape spots are not a disease. Spots are caused when cold water comes in contact with soil or foliage. Or if direct sunlight shines on wet leaves, spots may occur. These cannot be removed.
Treatment: Water or fertilizer solutions should be room temperature before applying to plants. If plant leaves become wet, remove plants from direct sunlight until leaves dry.

Pest and Disease Controls

GENERIC NAME	TRADE NAME	USES	REMARKS
Benomyl	Benlate	Botrytis blight, crown rot, powdery mildew	Fungicide. Non-toxic to humans.
Captan	Orthocide, Captan	Crown rot, powdery mildew	Fungicide. Non-toxic to humans.
Dicofol	Kelthane	Mites	Insecticide. Moderately toxic to humans.
Dimethoate	Cygon	Root nematodes, leaf mealy bugs, blackflies, plant lice, mites	Insecticide.
Ferbam	Ferbam	Crown rot, powdery mildew	Fungicide, non-toxic to humans. Black powder can stain leaves and flowers. Captan or benomyl are preferred.
Malathion	Cythion	Aphids, plant lice, leaf mealy bugs, whiteflies	Insecticide. Low toxicity to humans.
Sulfur	Sulfur, many	Crown rot, mildew	A widely used and well-known fungicide.

Diseases and Cultural Problems

Powdery mildew

Crown rot

Botrytis blight

Ring spot

Petiole rot

Green slime

Propagating Plants

African violets and the other gesneriads included in this book are easy to *propagate*—or produce new plants— by rooting plant parts or by starting plants from seeds. The ease with which they can be multiplied is one reason why African violets are popular.

Plants can be multiplied in a number of ways. Popular methods include rooting leaf cuttings in soil and water, dividing existing plants and starting plants from seeds. The combination of different soil mixes, planting mediums, light and other factors creates a large number of variables. The following discusses basic materials and procedures.

PROPAGATION BASICS

Timing—Spring is the best time of year to propagate African violets. Light conditions are bright and even. In addition, this is when plants are beginning a new growth spurt. But successful propagation can also be achieved at any time of the year.

Temperature—65F (19C) is the minimum for successful propagation from plant parts, such as cuttings. If home temperatures fall below this level, wait until warmer weather to propagate. Conditions should be warmer if growing seeds—72F to 75F (22C to 24C).

Planting Mediums—Leaf and stem cuttings, suckers and seeds are propagated in various materials and soil mixes called *planting*

Left: It is easy to multiply African violets to increase your collection. Above: New growth emerges from base of leaf propagated in soil mix.

mediums. These include horticultural vermiculite, perlite and standard African violet soil mix.

Horticultural vermiculite is a sterile, mica product, usually available in bags at garden-supply stores. Expert growers often recommend using horticultural vermiculite. Perlite is a lightweight, sterile product. It is also available from garden-supply stores. African violet soil mixes can be purchased or you can make your own. Some simple recipes are listed on page 12. Another mix that works well is equal parts of horticultural vermiculite or perlite mixed with sphagnum peat moss.

It is recommended that you treat planting mediums, cuttings and implements with fungicides and disinfectants to prevent fungal diseases. This is particularly true when starting from seeds. Benomyl fungicide is commonly used to treat plants. Rubbing alcohol is used to sterilize implements such as tweezers and scissors.

Containers and Flats—Plastic pots, clay pots and flats designed for propagating are commonly used to hold planting mediums. But many household items can be recycled as containers. These include paper and styrofoam cups, plastic butter tubs, plastic containers and milk jugs.

Plastic and clay pots usually have drainage holes. If you recycle plastic household containers such as butter tubs or milk jugs, you'll have to make holes yourself. Heat a screwdriver or ice pick over a flame. When tip is hot, gently push through bottom of container in several places to make holes. Punch holes through bottom of milk carton with ice pick, scissors or knife.

Sterilize containers before use. Soak in a solution of 1 part household bleach to 10 parts water for about 10 minutes. Rinse container with clean, clear water. If clay pots are used, soak them in bleach solution for at least two hours to allow solution to penetrate pourous clay. Rinse with clear water.

Implements—Items such as a razor blade, knife, tweezers and cuticle scissors are used to remove leaves and suckers for propagation. Sterilize them before use by dipping into rubbing alcohol.

INCREASE YOUR COLLECTION: SWAP BY MAIL

New plants can be purchased from nurseries, supermarkets or flower shops. You can also trade plants and leaf cuttings with friends. Many mail-order outlets offer plants or leaves by mail.

One of the most economical ways is to trade by mail with other enthusiasts. By joining African violet and gesneriad societies, you can obtain names and addresses of people interested in swapping leaves and plants. A listing of societies is provided on page 141.

Avoid mailing leaves during the winter months because of potential damage from cold. Summer heat may also cause damage to leaves. Spring or fall are best times for mailing.

1. Prepare a leaf for mailing by cutting the petiole longer than normal for propagation. The recipient can then trim end of stem if it has dried out.
2. Enclose lower one-third of stem in a moisture-holding material such as cotton or tissue. Cover tissue with aluminum foil or plastic wrap to maintain moisture around the stem. Place leaf in a plastic freezer bag and seal.
3. To prevent damage to the leaf during transit, use a mailing tube or small box. Place crinkled newspaper in the box as a cushion.
4. Place plastic freezer bag in the container and add more packing material. The packing prevents the leaf from moving around in the container.

Propagating African Violets and Other Gesneriads

	Seeds	Stem Cuttings	Leaf Cuttings	Stolons	Tubers	Rhizomes
Achimenes	•	•	•			•
Aeschynanthus	•	•	•			
Agalmyla	•	•	•			
Alloplectus	•	•				
Chirita	•	•	•			
Codonanthe	•	•				
Columnea	•	•				
Episcia	•	•	•	•		
Gesneria	•	•				
Gloxinia	•	•	•		•	
Kohleria						
Koellikeria	•	•	•			•
Nautilocalyx	•	•	•		•	
Nematanthus	•	•				
Neomortonia	•	•				
Petrocosmea	•		•			
Saintpaulia (African violets)	•	•	•			
Sinningia	•	•	•		•	
Smithiantha	•	•	•			•
Streptocarpus	•	•	•			

Rooting Leaf Cuttings in Soil Mix

1. Select container with drainage holes. Scrub in hot, soapy water then rinse in clear water. Place 2 inches of sterilized (pasteurized) planting medium in container. Moisten soil with fungicide solution to prevent fungal infections. Benomyl or captan are commonly used. Allow soil to drain.

2. Sterilize sharp knife, cuticle scissors or razor blade by dipping in rubbing alcohol. Select medium-size, firm, healthy leaf with stem that is 1-1/2 to 2 inches long from interior of plant. Leaves from plant center tend to root more quickly and more often than outside leaves. Slice through leaf stem at a 45° angle. Or slit leaf up middle about 1/2 inch after removing from plant.

3. Put leaf aside for several hours or overnight. Cut will heal and form callus over wound. Dip stem in rooting hormone powder containing fungicide. Tap off excess powder. Apply benomyl or captan with an artist's brush to cut on parent plant.

4. Use pencil to make holes in planting medium. Bury stem end in medium to 1/4 inch from leaf base. Firm medium around stem to make good contact. Insert toothpicks in medium to hold leaves off medium to prevent rot. Label stem according to variety.

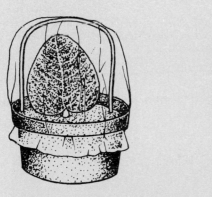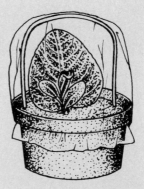

5. Cover container with plastic wrap to conserve moisture and increase humidity. Keep plastic out of contact with leaves by making a support out of wire. Or invert clear plastic glass or glass jar over stem and leaf. Set in room with bright light but no direct sun. Three days later, open plastic or glass cover to allow air circulation. Leave slightly open after that. If moisture condenses on cover, wipe it off.

6. New *plantlets*—tiny plants—will emerge from developing root system in 3 to 6 weeks. Remove cover when plantlets are evident. Water and feed with quarter-strength liquid fertilizer. Thereafter, feed once a month with half-strength fertilizer until plants are established.

7. When plantlets are about 3/4 inch high, cut off parent leaf, separate plantlets and plant each in 2-1/4-inch pot. Prior to planting, scrub pots with hot, soapy water and rinse with clear water. Care for new plants the same as established plants.

8. When plant leaves extend beyond 2-1/4-inch pot, transplant to 4-inch pot. Plants should bloom in 9 to 12 months.

Rooting Leaf Cuttings in Water

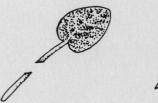

1. Use sharp, sterilized knife or razor blade to remove medium-size, firm, healthy leaves that have stems 1 to 2 inches long. Avoid taking leaves from outer edge of plant. They usually don't root as easily as leaves from plant's interior.

2. Slice through leaf stem at a 45° angle. Put leaf aside for several hours or overnight. This allows cut to heal and form a callus.

3. Sterilize clear glass by washing in hot, soapy water. Place activated charcoal in bottom. Fill with tap water. Cover top of glass with aluminum foil. Punch holes in foil and place leaf stems through holes so they are in water. Top-heavy leaves may fall over, causing stems to lift out of water. Avoid by using small glass, placing leaf so side of glass supports leaf.

4. If leaf shows signs of rot—tip of cutting is brownish and mushy—remove from water. Change water and allow healthy cuttings to continue root development.

5. Roots should be visible in 2 to 6 weeks and small plantlets will form. When roots are approximately 1/3 inch long, pot new plants in sterile, 2-1/4-inch containers. See Rooting Leaf Cuttings in Soil Mix, Step 7, page 37.

6. After newly planted stems become established, a number of small plantlets will grow around plant leaf. When leaves of plantlets are about one-third as long as leaves of the parent plant, remove them from pot. Separate young plants and plant each in a pot.

Option: Fill bowl with enough sterilized pebbles or stones to support leaf stems. Insert stems among pebbles or stones. Add water and maintain level to keep ends of stems moist, but leaves dry. When plantlets are about 1 inch high, pot as described above.

Propagation by Suckers

Suckers are tiny plantlets that grow from base of leaves. When removed, they grow into new plants. Select suckers of manageable size before propagation. They are easier to handle than small cuttings.

1. Sterilize sharp knife, razor blade or sharp scissors and remove suckers from parent plant. Leaves should be at least 1-1/2 inches long, preferably longer.

2. Apply captan or benomyl fungicide to cuts on parent plant and cuttings to prevent disease. Dust ends of cuttings with light coating of rooting hormone powder.

3. Plant cuttings in 3-inch pots filled with African violet soil mix or similar planting medium. Place pot in bright, sunny window out of direct sunlight. Keep soil moist but not soggy until plant is established.

Propagation by Division

Mature African violet plants often produce two or more crowns. If divided, each crown can become new plant. The best time to divide crowns is just after bloom, when each crown begins producing new leaves.

1. Allow soil to dry before dividing crowns. Wet soil sticks to roots and makes it difficult to see natural division of crowns.

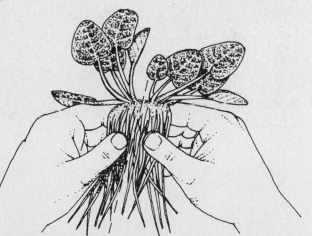

2. Remove plant and rootball from pot. Gently shake most of soil from roots. Look closely for natural division. Carefully pull crowns apart to see if substantial root system exists on each one. You may have to use sharp, sterilized knife to separate them.

3. Dust cuts or open wounds with fungicide and with rooting hormone powder.

4. Plant each crown in 3-inch pot with fresh, sterilized African violet mix. Place pots in bright, sunny window out of direct sunlight. Water plants lightly during first 3 weeks. After plants have recovered and become established, plant each in 4-inch pot.

Propagation from Seeds

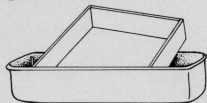

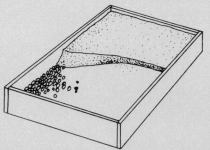

1. Prepare 3-inch-deep containers or flats. Scrub with hot, soapy water and rinse. Then place in solution of 1 part household bleach to 10 parts water for 5 minutes. Rinse with clear water.

2. Place layer of sterilized drainage material such as pebbles, activated charcoal or several thicknesses of absorbent paper towels in bottom of container. Add 2 inches of sterilized, fast-draining planting medium. If you use African violet soil mix, add 1 part horticultural vermiculite to 2 parts mix.

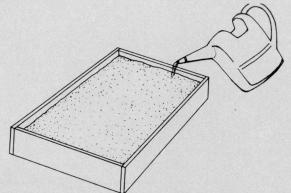

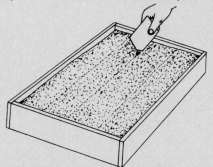

3. Drench container and soil with fungicide solution such as benomyl or captan. Allow water to drain. Press down lightly on medium to remove excess water.

4. African violet seeds and those of most other gesneriads are miniscule, resembling dust. Select windless place when sowing seeds. Sow seeds in rows directly from package. Or mix with small quantity of sterilized sand to provide more even distribution of seeds. Do not cover seeds with medium. Lightly press them into medium with your fingers.

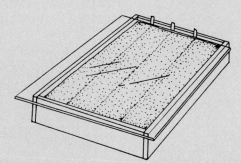

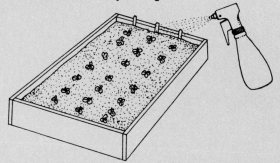

5. Label rows of seeds. Cover container with clear plastic or glass. Place in warm place, about 75F to 85F (24C to 30C). Provide bright light but not direct sunlight. As moisture accumulates, wipe dry. Seed germination is erratic. Some germinate in only 2 weeks; others may take several months.

6. After seeds germinate, remove plastic or glass cover. Keep seedlings in bright light. If grown under artificial light, place containers so seedlings are 3 to 4 inches below lights. Never allow planting medium to dry out. Keep damp but don't overwater. Misting is ideal way to provide moisture.

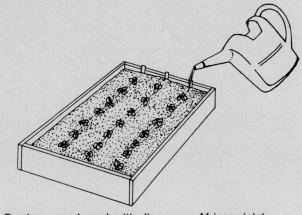

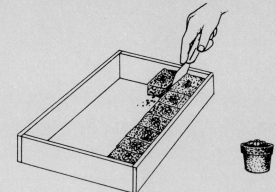

7. Feed once each week with all-purpose African violet fertilizer, diluted one-quarter strength. Watch for mold or fungus growing on soil surface. At first sign, treat soil with fungicide solution. After 2 weeks, begin program to prevent fungus diseases.

8. When seedlings are large enough to handle, transplant each in 2-1/4-inch pot. Use kitchen knife or putty knife to move soil and seedlings. Care for new plants the same as established plants.

CREATING HYBRIDS

Pollen for hybridizing can be collected from anthers with an artist's brush.

Many African violet enthusiasts enjoy creating new varieties. The most common way is through *hybridization.* This is the process of producing a new plant—a hybrid—by crossing or breeding two plants with different genetic backgrounds.

Although the process of hybridizing is simple, the reasons for the resulting appearance of hybrid plants are complex. It requires understanding the basic principles of the science of *genetics.* Genetics is the branch of biology that deals with heredity and variation in related plants and animals. Four terms you should know and understand are:

Chromosomes—Microscopic, rod-shape bodies that carry the *genes* that convey hereditary characteristics. The number of chromosomes in each living thing is constant and specific for each species.

Genes—Microscopic units carried at specific points on chromosomes. Genes transmit and determine hereditary characteristics of offspring.

Dominant Traits—Hereditary characteristics that are dominant and visible in the offspring.

Recessive Traits—Hereditary characteristics in plants that are dominated or controlled by dominant traits, and are not usually visible in the offspring. Recessive traits may be visible in future generations.

The genetic history of any new variety of African violet is complex. Color, foliage, shape, size and vigor of plant and flower type result from generations of breeding. The fascination of hybridizing is the unpredictability of the results when any two varieties are crossed.

STRUCTURE OF AN AFRICAN VIOLET FLOWER

Before attempting to hybridize your own varieties, you should know the basic anatomy of an African violet flower. African violets are *bisexual,* having both male and female organs on the same plant. Botanists call these *perfect plants.* The best way to learn about the flower's structure is to examine it closely. See photo, page 42.

African violet blossoms have five *lobes,* or petals. In addition to petals, yellow sacs are located in the middle of the flower. These sacs are called *anthers.* They contain dustlike *pollen*—the male fertilizing agent. Short, yellow filaments attach the anthers to the flower.

The female part of the blossom also projects from the center of the flower. The female organ is called the *pistil.* The slender filament is called the *style.* At the top end of the style is an enlarged tip called the *stigma.* At the base end of the pistil are slightly enlarged *ovaries.* Ovaries lie beneath the flower at the end of the stem. They contain immature *ovules,* seeds that can become fertilized.

The stigma becomes sticky after a flower has bloomed for several days. It remains sticky for several hours after petals drop. Fertilization takes place while the stigma is sticky. The pollen from the anther adheres to the stigma, then moves down the pistil to the ovaries, fertilizing the immature ovules.

At the bottom of the flower, beneath the petals, are five green *sepals*. These are the outer layer of leaves that protect the flower during bud stage. Later on, they protect the developing seed pod.

In natural habitats, insects usually transfer pollen from anthers to the stigma. To hybridize or cross flowers, you must transfer the pollen from the anther of one variety to the stigma of another variety. Artist's brushes and pipe cleaners are commonly used to transfer pollen. A step-by-step process is described on the following page.

When hybridized plants bloom, you will see the results of your work. If you crossed two plants with attractive characteristics, the result may be an exceptionally beautiful and unique new variety. The chances of producing an outstanding new variety are slim, but it does happen. Keep track of the results of the crosses you make. If you like the cross, keep the seeds. If plants are not that attractive and you don't like the cross, dispose of them.

You may want to register your new hybrid plant with the African Violet Society of America. For further information, write to African Violet Society, P.O. Box 1326, Knoxville, TN 37901.

Structure of an African Violet Flower

Stigma

Style

Pistil

Anther

Ovary

Petal

How to Hand-Pollinate Flowers

Entire cycle from pollination to ripe seeds usually takes 6 to 9 months. Flowers to be crossed should be mature—not past prime or recently opened.

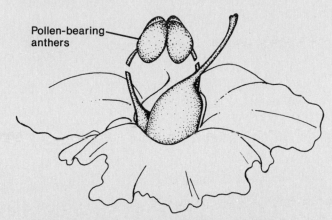

Pollen-bearing anthers

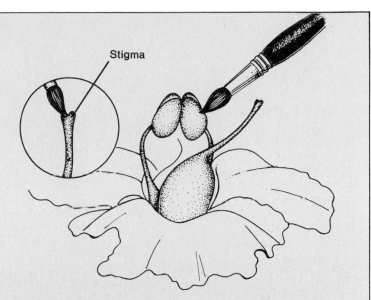

Stigma

1. Experts recommend that pollen-bearing anthers be removed from female parent plant before buds open. This avoids accidental self-fertilization of plants. If not removed, anthers could burst open. *Thrips,* a common insect pest, can fertilize flowers, ruining your hybridizing attempt.

2. Transfer pollen from anthers of male parent to stigma of female parent. There are several ways to do this:
Method A: Use a small artist's paintbrush, about 1/8 inch across. Place on male anther until some pollen adheres to brush. Transfer pollen to female stigma of parent plant.

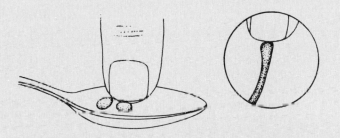

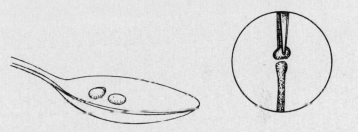

Method B: Cut section of male anthers into spoon or onto piece of paper. Place thumbnail on anther until pollen adheres. Brush thumbnail across stigma of female parent plant.

Method C: Snip off male anthers of plant with sharp cuticle scissors. Place spoon or piece of paper beneath to catch anthers. Pick up an anther with tweezers and rub it on female stigma of parent plant.

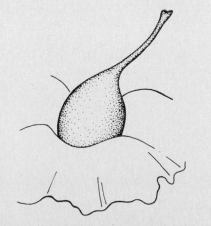

4. Keep a record of fertilized plants. Experienced growers tie a small tag on hybridized plants indicating male parent, female parent and date hybridization took place. Male parent is listed first; female parent is listed second. Tag should look like this:

LIGHT GIANT
x
MY DESIRE
6/15/83

3. If fertilization is successful, ovaries and seed capsule will swell. This usually occurs in 7 to 14 days. Capsule will continue to swell for 6 to 9 months until seeds ripen. When stem and seed capsule turn brown and begin to shrivel, remove seed capsule from stem. Place capsule on dish or jar lid. Set in warm, sunny spot to dry.

5. Plant seeds, following instructions for Propagating from Seeds, page 40. Plant seeds immediately after seed capsule is removed from plant. Or wait for 1 month until after seeds have dried. You can wait as long as 1 year before planting.
Seeds germinate over a long period. Don't be surprised if some seedlings emerge after 3 or 4 weeks. Others may take up to 4 months. Seed pods ripen in a variety of shapes and sizes.

Displaying & Showing African Violets

What could be a more welcome addition to your home's interior than a never-ending supply of flowering plants? After you have established your African violet collection, you will be able to use their natural beauty to add cheer to your "interiorscape." An extensive range of flower colors is available to match your home decor. Pinks, whites, blues, purples and reds add the perfect dash of color to any room in your house.

AFRICAN VIOLETS AS ACCENTS
To have African violets on hand as decorative complements, many hobbyists care for dozens of plants in one growing area. This area is usually in an out-of-the-way location, such as the basement or spare bedroom. Conditions are arranged to simplify their care. Fluorescent lights and watering mats are often used. Then, as plants come into bloom, they are placed around the house as decorative accents.

Any room is more attractive when dressed up with lovely, blooming plants. In the bathroom, place them on the vanity or in containers hung on walls. Favorite kitchen objects can serve as containers, bringing color and greenery to the cooking area. Plants can be showcased in the living room as accents on coffee tables, end tables or as complements to favorite porcelains. During winter when cut flowers from the garden are unavailable, several plants can be grouped together to make a dramatic centerpiece for the dining table.

PLANT DISPLAYS
Plant stands, available in most garden centers, department stores or discount stores, are popular ways to display plants. These are available in a wide range of prices and materials, from plastic, wood and painted metal to elegant brass, chrome and glass. Antique Victorian wicker stands make attractive display pieces. Brass planter poles, bakers' stands and hanging window shelves can also be used.

Because of their small, uniform size, African violets can be displayed in any room of your home. The following pages provide some ideas for displaying these beautiful and interesting house plants.

Left: Group of several plants on display stand creates focal point in a room. Above: A few plants on a bright windowsill is a simple way to grow African violets.

Left: African violets adapt to creative displays. Wicker bread basket serves as decorative tray for half-dozen plants.
Below: Windowsill perch is traditional spot for African violets. Colored bottles add interesting effect. Fill bottles with water and humidity around plants will be increased as water evaporates.

Opposite page, top: Potted African violets are placed in baskets to bring color and greenery to bathroom.
Below left: African violet was chosen for blossom color to accent wallpaper. The many different flower colors available make it easy to use African violets as decorative elements.
Below right: Small African violet as table centerpiece adds an elegant touch.

GLASS GARDENS

Miniature and semiminiature African violets and other gesneriads are excellent grown in glass containers. These containers make decorative additions to the home. Aquarium tanks, brandy snifters, old pickle jars and cider jugs make interesting and attractive homes for African violets.

One advantage of growing African violets in glass gardens is increased humidity. Water vapor from plants condenses on the inside surface of glass, creating a humid, mini-environment. "Closed" gardens such as bottle gardens recycle most water given to plants, so watering is seldom required. Open containers such as aquariums or glass bowls require water more often but not as much as a clay or plastic pot. For these reasons, terrariums and glass containers are recommended for growing gesneriads in arid, low-humidity regions.

Miniature African violets are prime candidates for glass gardens. They require small pots to grow properly, which tend to dry out rapidly when grown in open air. Soil dries out at a slow rate in a glass container, so proper moisture levels are easier to maintain.

Miniature Landscapes—African violets can be combined with other small house plants to create miniature landscapes in glass containers. Include plants such as dwarf fern, baby's tears, creeping fig, miniature begonias and various lichens, mosses and liverworts.

Be artistic in creating glass gardens. Fashion small hills and valleys in planting soil. Insert stones or attractive pieces of weathered wood in appropriate locations around plants. Fernbark will simulate small logs. Use fine gravel to create dry stream beds. Many of these materials are available in aquarium shops and pet stores.

If you add these materials to your glass garden, be sure to sterilize them. If not, your plants can soon become infected with disease or pests. Be especially careful with wood, rocks or other items gathered from the wild. Place materials in rubbing alcohol, then rinse with clear water before adding to container.

Caution—These containers have no drainage, and recycle their water. A little water goes a long way, so it is easy to overwater plants. Water sparingly until you get a feel for the water requirements of plants in these containers.

Planting a Bottle Garden

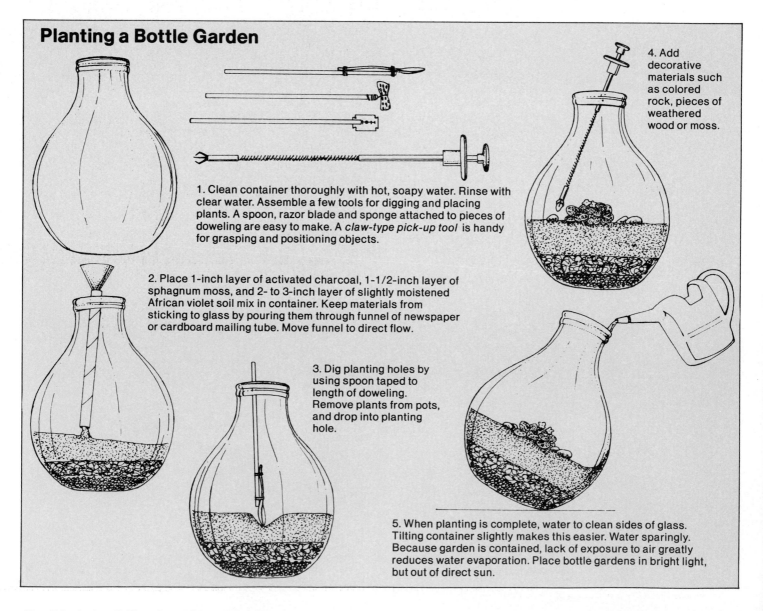

1. Clean container thoroughly with hot, soapy water. Rinse with clear water. Assemble a few tools for digging and placing plants. A spoon, razor blade and sponge attached to pieces of doweling are easy to make. A *claw-type pick-up tool* is handy for grasping and positioning objects.

2. Place 1-inch layer of activated charcoal, 1-1/2-inch layer of sphagnum moss, and 2- to 3-inch layer of slightly moistened African violet soil mix in container. Keep materials from sticking to glass by pouring them through funnel of newspaper or cardboard mailing tube. Move funnel to direct flow.

3. Dig planting holes by using spoon taped to length of doweling. Remove plants from pots, and drop into planting hole.

4. Add decorative materials such as colored rock, pieces of weathered wood or moss.

5. When planting is complete, water to clean sides of glass. Tilting container slightly makes this easier. Water sparingly. Because garden is contained, lack of exposure to air greatly reduces water evaporation. Place bottle gardens in bright light, but out of direct sun.

Bottle Gardens—Growing African violets and other house plants inside of a large, narrow-neck bottle is a real challenge. Bottles used for distilled water are commonly planted. Special tools and techniques are required to get plants into place. To keep materials from sticking to the inside of the glass requires care. Make a funnel out of newspaper, or use a cardboard mailing tube or tube from wrapping paper. Place the funnel into the neck of the bottle, and pour in the materials, moving the funnel to direct flow. You can use an item called a *claw-type pick-up tool* to grasp and position plants. These tools are inexpensive, and can usually be purchased at auto-supply stores. Kitchen spoons and other utensils can also be used to move plants about. Tape utensils to a length of doweling long enough to reach the bottom of the container.

Another method is to scatter seeds of standard African violets over planting soil. As the seedlings grow, remove all but three of the strongest plants. Plants should be positioned near the center of the bottle. Allow plants to grow and bloom. Select the best one and remove the other two plants. Use long tongs to pull plants out of the bottle. Allow selected plant to grow to maturity. Place bottle gardens in bright light, but out of direct sun.

THE VERTICAL DIMENSION

Displaying African violets in hanging pots and baskets is a striking way to feature plants in the home. Trailing varieties are well adapted to such culture. Standard African violets are also dramatic when displayed at eye level.

Many kinds of hanging containers are available. One of the most popular is a plastic container with a built-in saucer attached to catch water runoff. Clay pots, glazed and unglazed, are also used. Regardless of the type, make sure baskets or pots have drainage holes.

Wire baskets and redwood containers can be used to grow African violets. These containers are usually unsuitable for indoor use because they drip water on the floor. They can be used over tile floor or for outdoor displays.

Wire baskets and redwood containers must first be lined with sphagnum moss before adding planting soil. Moss and wire act as a container for soil and plant. After the basket is lined, add soil mixture or planting medium.

The Beldon basket is a popular container. Standard varieties can be planted on top. Trailing varieties are inserted in holes on sides. An attached saucer catches water runoff from watering.

Bottle garden planted with African violets and other house plants is an interesting way to bring greenery into the home. Because most water and nutrients are recycled inside glass, bottle gardens require little care after plants are established.

Displaying & Showing African Violets   49

A winning entry: The result of proper growing conditions, regular care and a little pampering.

African violet shows provide an opportunity for enthusiasts and growers to see hundreds of carefully nurtured and groomed specimens at peak bloom. Joining an African violet society and entering plants in competition can be satisfying, especially if you raise an award-winning specimen.

JUDGING AT SHOWS

At most African violet shows, specimen plants are judged according to five general categories. These aspects and the corresponding scale of points have been established by the African Violet Society of America. The total possible is 100.

Judges inspect African violets for symmetry, *floriferousness*—quantity of bloom—condition, size and type of blossom, and color. Points are awarded for each category. Awards given are for first, second and third place and honorable mention. The number of points awarded to a plant determines its eligibility for an award. See panel on the opposite page.

Leaf Pattern or Form—Leaf pattern or form of an African violet plant is the most important aspect when the judges start to count points. Spacing of leaves radially is considered. *Leaf mosaic,* leaves with little overlapping and vacant space between them, is desirable. It is considered an indication of proper training. If stems of lower leaves are long and there is space between them and the next tier of leaves, points will be deducted.

Floriferousness—This refers to the *quantity* of bloom. Number of flowers desired differs according to variety. Judges know the blooming habit of most varieties. Points are awarded according to the amount of bloom considered normal for that variety.

Condition—Refers to the general appearance and health of leaves. Points are deducted for imperfections. These include uneven green color, except in variegated leaves, brown edges, drooping leaves, ring spots, dust, insect and disease damage and bleached leaves. Presence of these factors indicate less than adequate care and improper growing conditions.

Size and Type of Blossom—Some varieties produce large blooms. Others produce small blooms. Blossoms are judged according to what is average for the variety.

Color—Refers to the ideal and accepted color of a specific variety. If color of bloom is bleached out or too dark, points are deducted. Ideal colors are usually produced if plant is given proper amount of light.

PREPARING AFRICAN VIOLETS FOR SHOWS

Following the planting and care guidelines in this book will help you produce African violet plants of show quality. In addition to normal cultural procedures, several steps are necessary to *train* plants for shows.

Symmetry of plants accounts for the most points given—30 points on a scale of 100. A major step toward symmetry is being sure young plants are centered in pots. Begin training plants when they have six leaves. Turn selected plants quarter-turn every other day regardless of whether they are grown under natural or artificial light. This helps ensure even, healthy growth.

Leaves sometimes grow irregularly, with uneven lateral spacing between them. You can gradually adjust the stem growth to produce more even spacing. Gently move the stem in the desired direction. Hold stem in place with toothpicks pushed into soil. Place toothpicks on side opposite direction you wish leaf to grow. Move stem and toothpicks about 1/4 to 1/2 inch every few days until symmetry is achieved. After several weeks, toothpicks can be removed from soil. Stems and leaves should remain in correct position.

Adjustments may also be necessary if one or more leaves fail to grow at same horizontal plane as others in the *rosette*—the circular arrangements of leaves of a plant. Use a bent piece of wire or a hairpin hooked over stem to lower or raise leaves to desired position. Or fashion a collar out of cardboard to maintain an equal horizontal level of leaves. Cut a circle out of a piece of cardboard. Circle should be about 2 inches larger than pot diameter. Cut a circle in center of this circle about half the diameter of pot. This makes a donut shape. Cut cardboard and fit it around crown and under leaves to support them. After several weeks, remove collar. The leaves should stay in place.

Getting Plants Ready for an African Violet Show

Adjusting Leaves for Symmetry

  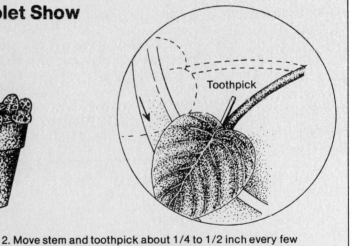

1. Leaves of African violets do not always grow with even spacing between them. To adjust stem growth for desirable symmetry, gently move stem in desired direction. Hold stem in place with toothpick pushed into soil.

2. Move stem and toothpick about 1/4 to 1/2 inch every few days until desired spacing is achieved. Leave toothpick in position for several weeks, then remove toothpick. Stems and leaves should remain in position.

Adjusting Horizontal Level of Plant

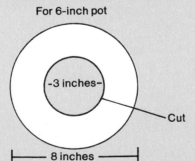

For 6-inch pot

-3 inches-

Cut

8 inches

Collar

1. A cardboard collar helps adjust leaves so they grow on same horizontal plane. Cut circle 2 inches wider than pot diameter. In center of circle cut another circle half the pot diameter. This makes a donut shape.

2. Fit collar around crown and under leaves of plant. This provides support for leaves. Remove collar after several weeks. Leaves should remain in same horizontal position.

Remove all *suckers,* small leaves or groups of leaves, before they get too large and interfere with plant symmetry.

Floriferousness is the second most important quality of a show plant—25 points possible. Here are a few tricks to increase bloom.

Disbudding—removing buds before they open—is used by experienced growers to force an abundance of blossoms at showtime. Normally, double-flowering varieties are disbudded about 10 weeks before a show. Single-flowering varieties are disbudded about 8 weeks before a show. It is also easier to train leaves to symmetry without a multitude of flower stalks.

Some plants may bloom too early or too late for show. For future reference, keep notes on when plants were disbudded and the resulting bloom.

Approximately 8 weeks before showtime, install new fluorescent tubes and increase light time to 14 hours a day.

A day or two before showtime, spruce up your plants. Clean the outside and inner rim of each pot. Remove all training aids such as hairpins, toothpicks and collars. Remove all dead or fading flowers, leaf stalks and seed pods. Use a cotton swab dipped in rubbing alcohol to remove any insects. Use an artist's brush to remove dirt particles from leaves.

TRANSPORTING PLANTS

Pack plants carefully when taking them to a show. If you don't, a sudden stop in an automobile or a dropped box can damage plants. All your time and effort in nurturing and grooming plants will have been in vain.

It is easy to make a carrying case for African violets. Use two cardboard boxes, one slightly smaller than the other, to hold plants while they are in transport. Cut round holes in the bottom of the smaller box. Make holes slightly smaller than the diameter of the pot rim. When you place pots in the holes, the box will support the pots by their rims. Pots should fit snugly. Place the smaller box, hole-side-up, in the larger box. Stuff newspaper in the spaces between the sides of the two boxes. Set pots in holes in the smaller box. Holes should be far enough apart so leaves do not touch each other or the sides of the larger box. Cover box with lid. If weather is cold, wrap box with blankets or be sure car heater is on. Cover carton with newspaper or a bedsheet to keep dust and warm, direct sunlight from plants.

GROOMING GUIDELINES

A checklist is helpful in preparing plants for show.
- ☐ Are secondary leaves symmetrical?
- ☐ Is neck of plant centered and vertical?
- ☐ Are petiole stubs removed?
- ☐ Are suckers removed?
- ☐ Are faded, damaged blossoms and bud stems removed?
- ☐ Are damaged leaves removed?
- ☐ Are insects removed?
- ☐ Is plant growing true to variety?
- ☐ Is plant centered in pot?
- ☐ Is plant potted at correct depth?
- ☐ Is foliage clean?
- ☐ Is pot clean?
- ☐ Have training aids such as toothpicks, supports and collars been removed?
- ☐ Does plant have desired single crown?
- ☐ Does plant have sufficient bloom?
- ☐ Is plant labeled with variety and your name?

How to Make a Transport Box

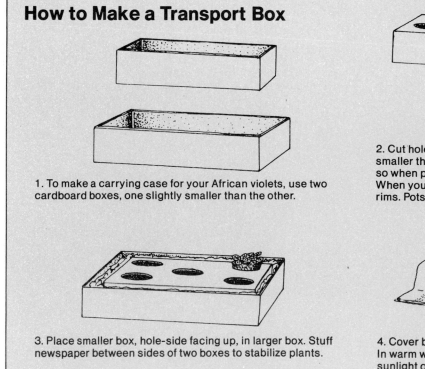

1. To make a carrying case for your African violets, use two cardboard boxes, one slightly smaller than the other.

2. Cut holes in bottom of smaller box. Make holes slightly smaller than diameter of pot rim. Space holes far enough apart so when plants are in position leaves will not touch each other. When you place pots in holes, box should support pots by their rims. Pots should fit snugly.

3. Place smaller box, hole-side facing up, in larger box. Stuff newspaper between sides of two boxes to stabilize plants.

4. Cover box with lid. In cold weather, wrap box with blankets. In warm weather, cover box with newspapers to keep dust and sunlight off plants.

A Close Look at an African Violet Show

This is a typical schedule for the amateur division of a New York State African Violet Society convention and show.

SECTION I—Specimen African Violets: Single Blossoms
    Class 1—Non-variegated foliage
    Class 2—Variegated foliage

SECTION II—Specimen African Violets: Semidouble and Double Blossoms
    Class 3—White, cream and blush
    Class 4—Light to medium pink
    Class 5—Dark pink and coral
    Class 6—Red, fuchsia and wine
    Class 7—Orchid and lavender
    Class 8—Light to medium blue
    Class 9—Dark blue and purple
    Class 10—Multicolor
    Class 11—Geneva (white edge only)
    Class 12—All other edged blossoms
    Class 13—Two-tone
    Class 14—Variegated foliage

SECTION III—Miniature Specimen African Violets
    Class 15—Single blossoms
    Class 16—Double blossoms
    Class 17—Variegated foliage

SECTION IV—Semiminiature Specimen African Violets
    Class 18—Single blossoms
    Class 19—Double blossoms
    Class 20—Variegated foliage

SECTION V—Specimen African Violets: Any Type or Color Blossoms, Any Foliage
    Class 21—Species
    Class 22—Seedlings
    Class 23—Sports and mutants
    Class 24—Grown in natural light
    Class 25—One or more African violets growing in an unusual, novel or decorative container. No other growing material permitted

SECTION VI—Specimen African Violets: Trailers
    Class 26—Standard
    Class 27—Miniature and semiminiature

SECTION VII—Specimen Plants: Gesneriads, other than African Violets. Protective Coverings Permitted
    Class 28—Miniature *Sinningia*
    Class 29—Any other miniature gesneriad
    Class 30—Tuberous gesneriad
    Class 31—Rhizomatous gesneriad
    Class 32—*Columneas*
    Class 33—*Nematanthus*
    Class 34—*Episcias*
    Class 35—*Streptocarpus*
    Class 36—Any other fibrous-rooted plant
    Class 37—Any non-blooming gesneriad grown primarily for foliage

Creative Designs

In addition to single plant entries, there are usually divisions for plants in terrariums, artistic plantings and arrangements. Often a theme is chosen and growers design their entries around it. Examples of themes are "Along the Briny Beach," a seashore design, and "Indian Summer," use of autumn foliage with African violet plants. Sometimes cut-flower arrangements are judged.

Winning entries at a typical African violet show.

Encyclopedia of African Violets

One of the appealing aspects of African violets is the number of varieties to choose from. There are thousands in cultivation, with variations in color, form and size to please any enthusiast. In this chapter, we feature descriptions of more than 100 of the most popular and available of these beautiful plants.

Some varieties are *patented*. This means that they are registered with the U.S. Patent and Trademark Office. Patented plants are indicated by the words Ballet, Rhapsodie or Optimara following the plant name. These varieties may not be propagated without permission or royalty payment to the original producer. Varieties that are not patented may be freely reproduced.

African violets can be grouped into three basic categories: *standard, miniature* and *semiminiature,* and *trailing.* Standard violets generally grow 8 to 10 inches wide, with some reaching 16 inches wide. They are the most common form.

Miniatures and semiminiatures are smaller and more compact. Semiminiatures grow 6 to 8 inches wide. Miniatures reach about 4 inches across. They are well adapted to growing in terrariums and glass containers. Be-

cause they are smaller than standard varieties, smaller pots are required. This decreases the amount of moisture available for humidity. By planting these plants in glass gardens, it is easy to maintain high humidity levels.

Trailing African violets have stems and leaves that drape over the pot rather than grow upright. Leaves and stems grow to about 10 inches long. They are best grown in hanging baskets.

ABOUT THE DESCRIPTIONS

In the following listings, varieties are described according to these categories:

Bloom Color—Several colors are available. They include white, pink, purple, violet, blue, red and many combinations. *Red* violets are not true red, but have a bluish tint. In the world of African violets, this color is referred to as red.

Bloom Shape—Variations include *violet type*—plain, single blooms—and *star-shape* blooms.

Bloom Type—Refers to petal characteristics. These include *plain* or *ruffled edge, single, double*—with additional set of petals—or *semidouble*—with a few more petals than a single.

Left: Many people think of violet-color blossoms when African violets are mentioned. This grouping shows off a few popular violet varieties. Above: Close-up view of 'New Brunswick', one of the popular Optimaras.

Leaf Color—Most are shades of green and blue-green. Some leaves have lighter or darker undersides in shades of green and reddish purple. Some have edges in contrasting colors. *Variegated leaves*— mottled or streaked with a lighter color—are also available.

Leaf Shape—Several shapes are available including plain leaf, sometimes called *boy type*. *Girl-type* leaves have a white spot at the leaf base. Others include *heart, oval, round* and *pointed*.

Leaf Type—Refers to the edges of the leaves and other leaf characteristics. Includes *plain edge, serrated, wavy, quilted texture* and *rippled*.

Growth Habit—Includes *standard*—slightly spreading—*upright* and *upright with sideways tendency*. *Trailing types* have leaves and stems that drape over the pot rim and grow downward.

BUYING PLANTS

African violet plants are commonly available in the house-plant department of supermarkets, at florists and nurseries. However, as violet hobbyists become more sophisticated, they often shop through mail-order outlets. Mail-order houses offer varieties rarely available at retail outlets. See page 141.

When your mail-order plants arrive, they may be somewhat wilted. This is usually nothing to worry about, because they normally revive in a few days. Place plants in a bright location, but away from direct sunlight. Water sparingly until plants adjust to their new environment.

If you purchase plants at a florist or supermarket, inspect the plants carefully before buying them. Avoid buying plants with spotted, stained or discolored leaves. Look for healthy, fresh, green foliage. Check stems, flowers, soil surface and undersides of leaves for pests and diseases. Buy only plants with a single crown. If possible, select plants that have symmetrical leaves. Finally, avoid buying plants at clearance sales. They are usually a close-out of a large selection, and are almost always inferior in quality. You'll have greater success with fresh, quality plants.

Plants for sale and in bloom have probably been grown in greenhouses under ideal conditions. Humidity is generally much higher in such an environment than in your home. Don't be alarmed if your plants fail to bloom again after you bring them home. They may require several months to adjust before blooming again.

Inside view at Hermann Holtkamp Greenhouses, a commercial grower, shows thousands of African violets, ready to be shipped to retail outlets.

Standard African Violets

'Alabama' Optimara

Bloom Color
Bicolor, white with blue

Bloom Shape
Violet type

Bloom Type
Single to semidouble with wavy edge

Leaf Color
Medium green with light-green underside

Leaf Shape
Heart

Leaf Type
Serrated

Growth Habit
Upright with slight sideways tendency

'Alberta' Optimara

Bloom Color
White with burgundy eye

Bloom Shape
Violet type

Bloom Type
Single to semidouble, multiflora. Parentage is tall, wild

Leaf Color
Dark green with light-green underside

Leaf Shape
Heart

Leaf Type
Slightly serrated

Growth Habit
Upright with sideways tendency

'Amazen Grace'

Bloom Color
White with pink flush

Bloom Shape
Violet type

Bloom Type
Single with ruffled edge

Leaf Color
Dark green

Leaf Shape
Heart

Leaf Type
Wavy with serrated edge

Growth Habit
Standard

'Anna' Ballet

Bloom Color
Very pale pink

Bloom Shape
Violet type

Bloom Type
Single with fringed edge

Leaf Color
Dark green

Leaf Shape
Heart

Leaf Type
Slightly serrated

Growth Habit
Standard

'Arizona I' Optimara

Bloom Color
Bicolor, burgundy-red with white stripe

Bloom Shape
Violet type

Bloom Type
Single to semidouble

Leaf Color
Dark green with purple-green underside

Leaf Shape
Heart

Leaf Type
Slightly serrated

Growth Habit
Standard

'Arizona II' Optimara

Bloom Color
Deep red with prominent yellow stamens

Bloom Shape
Violet type

Bloom Type
Single

Leaf Color
Medium green

Leaf Shape
Oval

Leaf Type
Slightly serrated

Growth Habit
Upright with strong flower stems

'Arkansas' Optimara

Bloom Color
Red-purple

Bloom Shape
Violet type

Bloom Type
Single to semidouble with additional flower petals

Leaf Color
Dark green with deep-purple underside

Leaf Shape
Heart

Leaf Type
Serrated

Growth Habit
Upright with strong flower stems

'Artist's Dream'

Bloom Color
White with purple edge

Bloom Shape
Violet type

Bloom Type
Double with fringed edge

Leaf Color
Light green

Leaf Shape
Heart

Leaf Type
Wavy

Growth Habit
Upright

'Atlanta' Optimara

Bloom Color
White to peach, with deeper peach or violet at eye

Bloom Shape
Violet type

Bloom Type
Single

Leaf Color
Dark-green edge, bright green at center

Leaf Shape
Round

Leaf Type
Serrated

Growth Habit
Upright

'Barbara' Rhapsodie

Bloom Color
Deep purple

Bloom Shape
Star type

Bloom Type
Single with fringed edge

Leaf Color
Medium green

Leaf Shape
Heart

Leaf Type
Serrated

Growth Habit
Standard

'Berry Splash'

Bloom Color
Pink with fuchsia-speckled edge
Bloom Shape
Star type
Bloom Type
Double
Leaf Color
Cream and green variegated
Leaf Shape
Oval
Leaf Type
Serrated
Growth Habit
Vigorous

'Blue Border'

Bloom Color
White with blue border
Bloom Shape
Violet type
Bloom Type
Double
Leaf Color
Green and white variegated
Leaf Shape
Heart
Leaf Type
Wavy with serrated edge
Growth Habit
Standard

'Blue Fandango'

Bloom Color
Intense violet with white

Bloom Shape
Star type

Bloom Type
Double with fringed edge

Leaf Color
Medium green

Leaf Shape
Oval

Leaf Type
Wavy with serrated edge

Growth Habit
Standard

'Blue Tempest'

Bloom Color
Light blue

Bloom Shape
Star type

Bloom Type
Double

Leaf Color
Medium green

Leaf Shape
Oval

Leaf Type
Slightly serrated

Growth Habit
Standard

'Calais'

Bloom Color
Soft pink-white

Bloom Shape
Violet type

Bloom Type
Single with fringed edge

Leaf Color
Medium green

Leaf Shape
Heart

Leaf Type
Wavy and serrated

Growth Habit
Strong upright

'California' Optimara

Bloom Color
Purple-violet

Bloom Shape
Violet shape

Bloom Type
Single to semidouble

Leaf Color
Dark green with light-green
underside

Leaf Shape
Round-heart

Leaf Type
Serrated

Growth Habit
Upright

'Cameo Queen'

Bloom Color
White

Bloom Shape
Violet type

Bloom Type
Double

Leaf Color
Dark green with dark-red underside

Leaf Shape
Oval pointed

Leaf Type
Serrated

Growth Habit
Standard

'Candy Cane'

Bloom Color
White with deep-lavender center

Bloom Shape
Violet type

Bloom Type
Single with fringed edge

Leaf Color
Dark green

Leaf Shape
Heart

Leaf Type
Wavy and serrated

Growth Habit
Standard

'Carla' Ballet

Bloom Color
Deep pink with white edge
Bloom Shape
Violet type
Bloom Type
Single with fringed edge
Leaf Color
Dark green
Leaf Shape
Oval
Leaf Type
Slightly serrated
Growth Habit
Upright

'Claret Queen'

Bloom Color
Red with white edge
Bloom Shape
Star type
Bloom Type
Single
Leaf Color
Dark green
Leaf Shape
Heart
Leaf Type
Severely serrated
Growth Habit
Standard

'Colorado' Optimara

Bloom Color
Red
Bloom Shape
Violet type
Bloom Type
Single with frilled and wavy edge
Leaf Color
Medium green with purple-green underside
Leaf Shape
Heart
Leaf Type
Slightly serrated
Growth Habit
Upright

'Confessions'

Bloom Color
Pink, speckled with darker pink
Bloom Shape
Star type
Bloom Type
Double
Leaf Color
Dark green with darker-green underside
Leaf Shape
Oval
Leaf Type
Serrated
Growth Habit
Vigorous, upright

'Connecticut' Optimara

Bloom Color
Lilac

Bloom Shape
Violet type

Bloom Type
Single with slight tendency to semidouble

Leaf Color
Dark green with purple-green underside

Leaf Shape
Heart

Leaf Type
Slightly serrated

Growth Habit
Sturdy upright

'Coral Radiance'

Bloom Color
Deep pink

Bloom Shape
Violet type

Bloom Type
Single to semidouble

Leaf Color
Medium green

Leaf Shape
Oval

Leaf Type
Serrated

Growth Habit
Standard

'Crater Lake' Optimara

Bloom Color
Deep purple

Bloom Shape
Violet type

Bloom Type
Double

Leaf Color
Deep olive-green with traces of red-purple on underside

Leaf Shape
Round to heart

Leaf Type
Plain edge

Growth Habit
Upright with strong flower stems

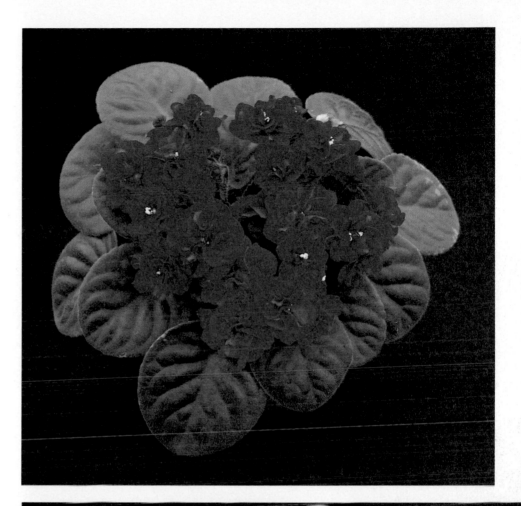

'Delaware' Optimara

Bloom Color
Burgundy-red

Bloom Shape
Star type

Bloom Type
Single to semidouble with 5 to 7 petals

Leaf Color
Medium green with light-green underside

Leaf Shape
Oval to heart shape

Leaf Type
Slightly serrated

Growth Habit
Upright with strong flower stems

'Dolly' Ballet

Bloom Color
White with violet markings

Bloom Shape
Violet type

Bloom Type
Double

Leaf Color
Medium green

Leaf Shape
Heart

Leaf Type
Serrated

Growth Habit
Standard

'Double Uncle Bob'

Bloom Color
Pink

Bloom Shape
Star type

Bloom Type
Double

Leaf Color
Dark green

Leaf Shape
Heart

Leaf Type
Smooth

Growth Habit
Standard

'Eileen's Pink'

Bloom Color
Light pink

Bloom Shape
Star type

Bloom Type
Double

Leaf Color
Medium green with rosy underside

Leaf Shape
Oval

Leaf Type
Slightly serrated

Growth Habit
Vigorous

'Erica' Ballet

Bloom Color
Fuchsia

Bloom Shape
Violet type

Bloom Type
Double with fringed edge

Leaf Color
Dark green

Leaf Shape
Heart

Leaf Type
Slightly serrated

Growth Habit
Standard

'Evelyn' Rhapsodie

Bloom Color
  Burgundy-blue

Bloom Shape
  Violet type

Bloom Type
  Single

Leaf Color
  Medium green with light-green underside

Leaf Shape
  Oval to heart shape

Leaf Type
  Slightly serrated

Growth Habit
  Upright with strong flower stems

'Fantasy Royal'

Bloom Color
  Blue, pink with blue spots

Bloom Shape
  Star type

Bloom Type
  Double

Leaf Color
  Medium green with light green underside

Leaf Shape
  Heart

Leaf Type
  Plain

Growth Habit
  Standard, vigorous

'Frosted Finesse'

Bloom Color
  Wine
Bloom Shape
  Violet type
Bloom Type
  Semidouble with fringed edge
Leaf Color
  Green and white variegated
Leaf Shape
  Oval
Leaf Type
  Plain edge
Growth Habit
  Standard

'Garnet Elf'

Bloom Color
  Fuchsia with white border
Bloom Shape
  Star type
Bloom Type
  Single with fluted edge
Leaf Color
  Dark green with dark-red
  underside
Leaf Shape
  Heart
Leaf Type
  Fluted edge
Growth Habit
  Small grower

'Georgia' Optimara

Bloom Color
Deep pink

Bloom Shape
Violet type

Bloom Type
Single

Leaf Color
Dark green

Leaf Shape
Heart

Leaf Type
Serrated

Growth Habit
Standard

'Glacier' Optimara

Bloom Color
White with light-cream stamens

Bloom Shape
Star type

Bloom Type
Single to semidouble

Leaf Color
Medium green with light-green underside

Leaf Shape
Round to heart

Leaf Type
Serrated

Growth Habit
Upright with strong flower stems

'Grace' Ballet

Bloom Color
Deep purple

Bloom Shape
Violet type

Bloom Type
Double with fringed edge

Leaf Color
Dark green

Leaf Shape
Heart

Leaf Type
Wavy with serrated edge

Growth Habit
Standard

'Hawaii' Optimara

Bloom Color
Intense royal blue with
silver-white edge

Bloom Shape
Star type

Bloom Type
Single with wavy edge

Leaf Color
Medium green with light-green
underside

Leaf Shape
Heart

Leaf Type
Serrated

Growth Habit
Upright with slight sideways
tendency. Mature flowers tend to
bend sideways

'Heidi' Ballet

Bloom Color
  Pink
Bloom Shape
  Star type
Bloom Type
  Single
Leaf Color
  Medium green
Leaf Shape
  Oval
Leaf Type
  Plain edge
Growth Habit
  Standard

'Helga' Ballet

Bloom Color
  Burgundy
Bloom Shape
  Violet type
Bloom Type
  Single
Leaf Color
  Medium green
Leaf Shape
  Oval
Leaf Type
  Plain edge
Growth Habit
  Standard

'Illinois' Optimara

Bloom Color
Pink with dark-pink eye

Bloom Shape
Star type

Bloom Type
Single to semidouble

Leaf Color
Medium green with light-green underside

Leaf Shape
Round

Leaf Type
Slightly serrated

Growth Habit
Upright with strong flower stems

'Indiana' Optimara

Bloom Color
Pink

Bloom Shape
Violet type

Bloom Type
Single

Leaf Color
Medium green with light-green underside

Leaf Shape
Oval

Leaf Type
Slightly serrated

Growth Habit
Upright with strong flower stems

'Jazzberry Pink'

Bloom Color
Pink

Bloom Shape
Star type

Bloom Type
Semidouble

Leaf Color
Dark green with light-green underside

Leaf Shape
Oval

Leaf Type
Pebbly leaf surface

Growth Habit
Standard

'Josie'

Bloom Color
Fuchsia with white edge

Bloom Shape
Star type

Bloom Type
Double

Leaf Color
Medium green with rosy underside

Leaf Shape
Heart

Leaf Type
Slightly serrated

Growth Habit
Vigorous

'Juliana'

Bloom Color
Intense red

Bloom Shape
Star type

Bloom Type
Semidouble

Leaf Color
Dark green with dark-red underside

Leaf Shape
Heart

Leaf Type
Wavy with serrated edge

Growth Habit
Standard

'Juliana' Rhapsodie

Bloom Color
White with violet markings

Bloom Shape
Star type

Bloom Type
Single

Leaf Color
Medium green

Leaf Shape
Heart

Leaf Type
Serrated

Growth Habit
Standard

'Kansas' Optimara

Bloom Color
Bicolor, white to deep pink with burgundy center

Bloom Shape
Star type

Bloom Type
Single with 5 to 7 petals

Leaf Color
Medium green with light-green underside

Leaf Shape
Heart

Leaf Type
Slightly serrated

Growth Habit
Upright with strong flower stems

'Kentucky' Optimara

Bloom Color
Light pink

Bloom Shape
Violet type

Bloom Type
Single

Leaf Color
Medium green with light-green underside

Leaf Shape
Oval to heart

Leaf Type
Slightly serrated

Growth Habit
Upright

'Leila's Blue'

Bloom Color
Blue

Bloom Shape
Star type

Bloom Type
Double with fringed edge

Leaf Color
Medium green with rosy underside

Leaf Shape
Heart

Leaf Type
Plain

Growth Habit
Upright, vigorous

'Light Giant'

Bloom Color
White and purple

Bloom Shape
Star type

Bloom Type
Semidouble

Leaf Color
Light green

Leaf Shape
Heart

Leaf Type
Serrated

Growth Habit
Standard

'Lisa' Ballet

Bloom Color
Pink and white

Bloom Shape
Star type

Bloom Type
Single

Leaf Color
Light green

Leaf Shape
Heart

Leaf Type
Pebbly leaf surface

Growth Habit
Standard

'Louisiana' Optimara

Bloom Color
Light pink

Bloom Shape
Violet type

Bloom Type
Single with frilled edge

Leaf Color
Dark green with purple-green
underside

Leaf Shape
Heart

Leaf Type
Slightly serrated

Growth Habit
Upright with slight sideways
tendency

'Lucy' Rhapsodie

Bloom Color
Intense lilac

Bloom Shape
Violet type

Bloom Type
Single to double

Leaf Color
Medium green with light-green underside

Leaf Shape
Round

Leaf Type
Smooth

Growth Habit
Upright with strong flower stems

'Manitoba' Optimara

Bloom Color
Light blue

Bloom Shape
Violet type

Bloom Type
Single, multiflora. Parentage is half-wild

Leaf Color
Medium green with purple-green underside

Leaf Shape
Heart

Leaf Type
Smooth

Growth Habit
Upright with slight sideways tendency

'Margit' Rhapsodie

Bloom Color
  Intense blue
Bloom Shape
  Violet type
Bloom Type
  Single
Leaf Color
  Medium green with light-green
  underside
Leaf Shape
  Heart
Leaf Type
  Smooth, small
Growth Habit
  Upright

'Mark Mahogany'

Bloom Color
  Deep red
Bloom Shape
  Star type
Bloom Type
  Double
Leaf Color
  Dark green with red underside
Leaf Shape
  Heart
Leaf Type
  Serrated edge
Growth Habit
  Standard

'Marta' Ballet

Bloom Color
Lavender

Bloom Shape
Violet type

Bloom Type
Double with fringed edge

Leaf Color
Dark green

Leaf Shape
Oval

Leaf Type
Slightly serrated

Growth Habit
Standard

'Maryland' Optimara

Bloom Color
Royal blue

Bloom Shape
Star type

Bloom Type
Single to semidouble

Leaf Color
Medium green with light-green underside

Leaf Shape
Heart

Leaf Type
Plain

Growth Habit
Upright with strong flower stems

'Massachusetts' Optimara

Bloom Color
Lilac with dark-lilac eye

Bloom Shape
Violet type

Bloom Type
Single to semidouble

Leaf Color
Medium green with light-green underside

Leaf Shape
Round to heart

Leaf Type
Smooth

Growth Habit
Upright

'Meta' Ballet

Bloom Color
Deep purple

Bloom Shape
Violet type

Bloom Type
Single

Leaf Color
Medium green

Leaf Shape
Heart

Leaf Type
Serrated edge

Growth Habit
Standard

'Michelle' Rhapsodie

Bloom Color
 Lilac
Bloom Shape
 Star type
Bloom Type
 Single
Leaf Color
 Medium green with bright-green underside
Leaf Shape
 Round
Leaf Type
 Slightly serrated
Growth Habit
 Upright with strong flower stems

'Ms. Pretty'

Bloom Color
 White with wide pink bands
Bloom Shape
 Violet type
Bloom Type
 Single with frilled edge
Leaf Color
 Dark green
Leaf Shape
 Oval
Leaf Type
 Serrated
Growth Habit
 Standard, vigorous

'My Desire'

Bloom Color
Pink

Bloom Shape
Star type

Bloom Type
Double

Leaf Color
Dark green

Leaf Shape
Heart

Leaf Type
Pebbly surface with serrated edge

Growth Habit
Standard

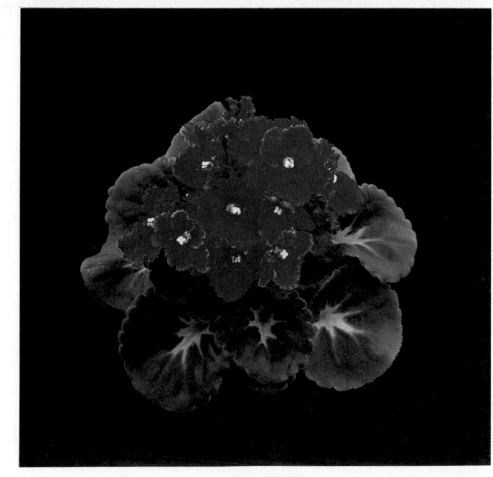

'Nashville' Optimara

Bloom Color
Red

Bloom Shape
Violet type

Bloom Type
Single with frilled edge

Leaf Color
Dark green with bright-green center, bright-green underside

Leaf Shape
Round

Leaf Type
Serrated and wavy

Growth Habit
Upright

'Nebraska' Optimara

Bloom Color
Bicolor, burgundy with whitish-purple frill

Bloom Shape
Violet type

Bloom Type
Semidouble

Leaf Color
Rich green with purple-green underside

Leaf Shape
Heart

Leaf Type
Wavy edge

Growth Habit
Upright with slight sideways tendency

'Nevada' Optimara

Bloom Color
Bicolor, white with red-purple edge

Bloom Shape
Violet type

Bloom Type
Single with frilled and wavy edge

Leaf Color
Medium green with bright-green underside

Leaf Shape
Round

Leaf Type
Slightly serrated

Growth Habit
Upright

'New Brunswick' Optimara

Bloom Color
Medium blue

Bloom Shape
Violet type

Bloom Type
Single to semidouble, multiflora. Parentage is half-wild

Leaf Color
Medium green with light-green underside

Leaf Shape
Round

Leaf Type
Smooth

Growth Habit
Upright with slight sideways tendency

'New Jersey' Optimara

Bloom Color
Intense pink

Bloom Shape
Violet type

Bloom Type
Single with frilled edge

Leaf Color
Medium green with light-green underside

Leaf Shape
Round to heart

Leaf Type
Smooth

Growth Habit
Upright with sturdy flower stems

'New Mexico' Optimara

Bloom Color
Bicolor, orchid with intense purple edge

Bloom Shape
Violet type

Bloom Type
Single with frilled edge

Leaf Color
Dark green with purple-green underside

Leaf Shape
Round

Leaf Type
Serrated

Growth Habit
Strong upright

'North Carolina' Optimara

Bloom Color
Deep burgundy-red

Bloom Shape
Violet type

Bloom Type
Single

Leaf Color
Medium green

Leaf Shape
Heart

Leaf Type
Slightly serrated

Growth Habit
Standard

'Ohio' Optimara

Bloom Color
Purple-red

Bloom Shape
Violet type

Bloom Type
Semidouble

Leaf Color
Dark green with purple-green underside

Leaf Shape
Round to heart

Leaf Type
Slightly serrated

Growth Habit
Strong upright

'Oklahoma' Optimara

Bloom Color
Burgundy-red with more intense eye

Bloom Shape
Violet type

Bloom Type
Single with wavy edge

Leaf Color
Dark green with purple-green underside

Leaf Shape
Round

Leaf Type
Slightly serrated

Growth Habit
Upright

'Ontario' Optimara

Bloom Color
White
Bloom Shape
Violet type
Bloom Type
Single to semidouble, multiflora
Leaf Color
Medium green with light-green underside
Leaf Shape
Oval to heart
Leaf Type
Plain
Growth Habit
Upright with sideways tendency

'Pamela' Rhapsodie

Bloom Color
Deep burgundy
Bloom Shape
Violet type
Bloom Type
Single to semidouble
Leaf Color
Dark green with purple-green underside
Leaf Shape
Heart
Leaf Type
Slightly serrated
Growth Habit
Upright with strong flower stems

'Pink Pippin'

Bloom Color
  Pink with white edge
Bloom Shape
  Violet type
Bloom Type
  Double
Leaf Color
  Dark green
Leaf Shape
  Oval
Leaf Type
  Slightly serrated
Growth Habit
  Standard

'Pink Ulli' Ballet

Bloom Color
  Bright pink
Bloom Shape
  Violet type
Bloom Type
  Double with fringed edge
Leaf Color
  Medium green
Leaf Shape
  Heart
Leaf Type
  Wavy with serrated edge
Growth Habit
  Standard

'Plum Frostee'

Bloom Color
Purple with edge that gradually changes from blue to white

Bloom Shape
Violet type

Bloom Type
Semidouble

Leaf Color
Medium green

Leaf Shape
Heart

Leaf Type
Serrated

Growth Habit
Sturdy upright

'Pom Pom Delight'

Bloom Color
Red

Bloom Shape
Violet type

Bloom Type
Double

Leaf Color
Dark green

Leaf Shape
Heart

Leaf Type
Fluted edge

Growth Habit
Standard

'Rhode Island'
Optimara

Bloom Color
Pink with dark-pink eye

Bloom Shape
Violet type

Bloom Type
Single with frilled edge

Leaf Color
Dark green with purple-green underside

Leaf Shape
Round

Leaf Type
Slightly serrated

Growth Habit
Upright

'Rio Rita'

Bloom Color
White with reddish-blue eye

Bloom Shape
Star type

Bloom Type
Single

Leaf Color
Light green

Leaf Shape
Heart

Leaf Type
Slightly serrated

Growth Habit
Standard

'Roxana' Rhapsodie

Bloom Color
White with red eye

Bloom Shape
Violet type

Bloom Type
Single

Leaf Color
Dark green

Leaf Shape
Heart

Leaf Type
Serrated

Growth Habit
Standard

'Royal Ruby'

Bloom Color
Deep fuchsia

Bloom Shape
Violet type

Bloom Type
Semidouble

Leaf Color
Medium green with dark-red
underside

Leaf Shape
Heart

Leaf Type
Slightly serrated

Growth Habit
Standard

'San Francisco'
Optimara

Bloom Color
Intense lilac

Bloom Shape
Star type

Bloom Type
Single to semidouble

Leaf Color
Dark green with bright-green center, purple-green underside

Leaf Shape
Round, girl-leaf type

Leaf Type
Serrated and wavy

Growth Habit
Upright

'Sherbet'

Bloom Color
Orchid and white

Bloom Shape
Star type

Bloom Type
Single

Leaf Color
Deep green

Leaf Shape
Heart

Leaf Type
Serrated

Growth Habit
Standard

'Smoky Mountains'
Optimara

Bloom Color
Pink
Bloom Shape
Violet type
Bloom Type
Semidouble with frilled edge
Leaf Color
Dark green with purple-green underside
Leaf Shape
Oval to heart
Leaf Type
Slightly serrated
Growth Habit
Upright with strong flower stems

'Snow Drift'

Bloom Color
White
Bloom Shape
Star type
Bloom Type
Single
Leaf Color
Medium green
Leaf Shape
Oval
Leaf Type
Serrated
Growth Habit
Upright, vigorous

'Sophia' Rhapsodie

Bloom Color
Intense blue-violet

Bloom Shape
Violet type

Bloom Type
Single with slightly wavy edge

Leaf Color
Dark green with purple-green underside

Leaf Shape
Heart

Leaf Type
Slightly serrated

Growth Habit
Upright with sturdy flower stems

'South Dakota' Optimara

Bloom Color
Pink

Bloom Shape
Violet type

Bloom Type
Single with frilled, wavy edge

Leaf Color
Dark green with purple-green underside

Leaf Shape
Oval to heart

Leaf Type
Slightly serrated

Growth Habit
Strong upright

'Sparkle Plenty'

Bloom Color
Pink with dark-pink edge

Bloom Shape
Violet type

Bloom Type
Double

Leaf Color
Medium green

Leaf Shape
Heart

Leaf Type
Serrated

Growth Habit
Standard

'Summer Lightning'

Bloom Color
White with purple edge

Bloom Shape
Violet type

Bloom Type
Single with slightly wavy edge

Leaf Color
Medium green

Leaf Shape
Oval

Leaf Type
Serrated

Growth Habit
Standard

'Swan Lake' Ballet

Bloom Color
Reddish blue

Bloom Shape
Violet type

Bloom Type
Single with fringed edge

Leaf Color
Dark green

Leaf Shape
Heart

Leaf Type
Serrated

Growth Habit
Standard

'Tawny Rose'

Bloom Color
Pink with white edge

Bloom Shape
Violet type

Bloom Type
Double

Leaf Color
Dark green

Leaf Shape
Heart

Leaf Type
Serrated

Growth Habit
Standard

'Tennessee' Optimara

Bloom Color
Bicolor, white marked with light to dark blue

Bloom Shape
Star type

Bloom Type
Single to semidouble

Leaf Color
Medium green

Leaf Shape
Round

Leaf Type
Slightly serrated

Growth Habit
Upright with strong flower stems

'Texas' Optimara

Bloom Color
Medium blue with prominent yellow stamens

Bloom Shape
Violet type, heavily ruffled

Bloom Type
Single to semidouble

Leaf Color
Dark green with light purple-green underside

Leaf Shape
Oval to heart

Leaf Type
Slightly serrated

Growth Habit
Upright with strong flower stems

'Unspoken'

Bloom Color
White with purple eye
Bloom Shape
Star type
Bloom Type
Double
Leaf Color
Light and dark green
Leaf Shape
Heart
Leaf Type
Plain
Growth Habit
Standard

'Utah' Optimara

Bloom Color
Intense blue-violet
Bloom Shape
Violet type
Bloom Type
Single to semidouble
Leaf Color
Dark green with purple-green
underside
Leaf Shape
Round
Leaf Type
Serrated
Growth Habit
Upright

'Vanessa' Rhapsodie

Bloom Color
Intense pink

Bloom Shape
Violet type

Bloom Type
Single to semidouble

Leaf Color
Medium green with purple-green underside

Leaf Shape
Round

Leaf Type
Smooth

Growth Habit
Compact, upright growth with slight sideways tendency

'Venetian Lace'

Bloom Color
White with lavender edge

Bloom Shape
Star type

Bloom Type
Double with fringed edge

Leaf Color
Light green

Leaf Shape
Heart

Leaf Type
Wavy with serrated edge

Growth Habit
Standard

'Washington'
Optimara

Bloom Color
Deep purple

Bloom Shape
Violet type

Bloom Type
Single to semidouble

Leaf Color
Dark green with purple-green underside

Leaf Shape
Round

Leaf Type
Serrated

Growth Habit
Upright with strong flower stems

'Wisconsin'
Optimara

Bloom Color
Deep purple

Bloom Shape
Violet type

Bloom Type
Single to semidouble, multiflora

Leaf Color
Medium green with light-green underside

Leaf Shape
Round

Leaf Type
Plain

Growth Habit
Upright with strong flower stems

'Wrangler's Stampede'

Bloom Color
Pink

Bloom Shape
Star type

Bloom Type
Double

Leaf Color
Variegated cream and green
with light-green underside

Leaf Shape
Heart

Leaf Type
Slightly serrated

Growth Habit
Vigorous

'Wyoming' Optimara

Bloom Color
Deep blue

Bloom Shape
Violet type

Bloom Type
Single to semidouble, multiflora

Leaf Color
Bright green with light-green
underside

Leaf Shape
Heart

Leaf Type
Slightly serrated

Growth Habit
Strong upright growth with
tendency to grow outward at
maturity

Miniature and Semiminiature African Violets

'Betcha'

Bloom Color
White with pencil-thin lilac edge

Bloom Shape
Violet type

Bloom Type
Double with fringed edge

Leaf Color
Medium to light green

Leaf Shape
Oval

Leaf Type
Serrated

Growth Habit
Semiminiature

'Joyful'

Bloom Color
White with red edge

Bloom Shape
Violet type

Bloom Type
Double with fluted edge

Leaf Color
Medium green

Leaf Shape
Heart

Leaf Type
Scalloped edge

Growth Habit
Compact miniature

'Love Bug'

Bloom Color
 Burgundy
Bloom Shape
 Star type
Bloom Type
 Semidouble with plain edge
Leaf Color
 Green and white variegated
Leaf Shape
 Oval
Leaf Type
 Plain edge
Growth Habit
 Miniature

'Wee Hope'

Bloom Color
 White with blue eye
Bloom Shape
 Star type
Bloom Type
 Semidouble
Leaf Color
 Glossy dark green
Leaf Shape
 Heart
Leaf Type
 Pebbly
Growth Habit
 Semiminiature

Trailing African Violets

'Buckeye Trails'

Bloom Color
White and deep red

Bloom Shape
Star type

Bloom Type
Double with fringed edge

Leaf Color
Medium green

Leaf Shape
Heart

Leaf Type
Plain

Growth Habit
Semiminiature trailer

'Snowy Trail'

Bloom Color
White

Bloom Shape
Violet type

Bloom Type
Semidouble with plain edge

Leaf Color
Light green

Leaf Shape
Heart

Leaf Type
Plain edge

Growth Habit
Semiminiature trailer

'Trails Delight'

Bloom Color
Rose

Bloom Shape
Violet type

Bloom Type
Single

Leaf Color
Green and white variegated

Leaf Shape
Heart

Leaf Type
Smooth edge

Growth Habit
Standard trailer

'Winding Trail'

Bloom Color
Medium blue and white

Bloom Shape
Violet type

Bloom Type
Double with plain edge

Leaf Color
Medium green

Leaf Shape
Heart and elongated

Leaf Type
Smooth edge

Growth Habit
Miniature trailer

African Violet Relatives

African violets have been a favorite house plant for many years. Their relatives, other *gesneriads,* are becoming more popular. Hundreds of species and varieties are grown, with more becoming available every year. Many are sold at florists and nurseries. After you have established your collection of African violets, you will probably want to experiment with some of their beautiful cousins.

Some gesneriads have special cultural needs, which are described in the individual descriptions. But most gesneriads share similar requirements in terms of light, water, soil, temperature, humidity and nutrients. If you are successful at growing African violets, you can succeed with the plants in this chapter.

One major difference exists between African violets and other gesneriads. Some varieties can be placed outdoors to decorate patios and porches during the warm, summer months. If you live in a mild climate, many of these plants can be grown outdoors all year long. Four are especially suited for growing in sheltered, outdoor areas: *Aeschynanthus, Columnea, Nematanthus* and *Kohleria.*

Blossoms and growth habits of gesneriads

In addition to African violets, other gesneriads are grown as house plants. Left: Gloxinias such as this 'Diana' type are prized for their magnificent blooms. Above: *Episcia* 'Chocolate Soldier' is grown for its striking foliage.

vary widely. Gloxinias, for example, sport large, velvety, bell-shape flowers. Colors range from brilliant, clear reds to purples, blues and whites. Foliage is handsome, velvety green. *Episcias* have brilliant, orange-red and scarlet flowers with green, silvery variegated and chocolate-brown leaves. *Achimenes* produce white, pink, blue, purple and red flowers. Varieties are available in erect, compact and trailing forms. *Streptocarpus,* common name cape primrose, is available as a patented series called *Bavarian Belle.* Colors include white, pink, red, blue and purple, with various color combinations. *Smithiantha,* common name temple bells, produces multicolored, tubular blossoms in red, orange, yellow, apricot, white and salmon.

Certain species are suited for growing in hanging baskets. *Aeschynanthus* sports brilliant, tubular flowers in reds, yellows and oranges. Foliage is a lush green, sometimes mottled, with gracefully trailing growth habit. *Columneas* have spectacular, tubular flowers in bright orange, red and yellow and color combinations. Foliage is also a rich green. *Nematanthus,* a more obscure variety, has pouchlike flowers, most of which are shades of orange. Some are mottled.

Achimenes
Magic Flower, Nut Orchid, Widow's Tear

Achimenes are native to the West Indies, Central America and Mexico. During the Victorian era, they were commonly grown as house plants. Their popularity declined after World War I. Because of the introduction of many beautiful hybrids, *Achimenes* are again being grown by many hobbyists.

Glossy, five-lobed flowers measure 1 to 2-1/2 inches across on stems almost 12 inches tall. Flowers are tubular to funnel shape. They bloom in a range of colors, including blue, white, pink, purple, red, yellow and pastel orange. Bloom period usually lasts from June to October. Plants grow 3 to 10 inches high. They go dormant in late October. Glistening foliage is hairy, medium green and grows 1 to 3 inches long.

There are two basic types of *Achimenes*—those with a pendulous, trailing habit and those with a bushy, upright habit. In mild-winter regions, *Achimenes* can usually be grown outdoors as perennials when given a northern or eastern exposure.

HOW TO PLANT
Purchase *scaly rhizomes,* rootlike cylindrical growths, usually 1/4 to several inches long. Scaly rhizomes are produced underground each year at the base of plant. You can also purchase plants or start plants from seeds. Plants or scaly rhizomes can be ordered from mail-order nurseries. Most nurseries have plants available in spring after danger of frost has passed.

For a showy, full-leaved display, plant five or six scaly rhizomes in a pot filled with growing medium. A commercial African violet soil mix is commonly used. Cover rhizomes with 1/2 to 1 inch of medium. Keep soil moist until plants sprout. For instructions on growing plants from seeds, see page 40.

LIGHT
Direct sun is too strong. Place in a south or east window receiving bright, indirect sunlight. Because they are summer-flowering plants, *Achimenes* can also be grown outdoors in summer under a lattice, arbor or porch shaded from direct sunlight.

If you grow *Achimenes* under artificial light, give them 14 to 16 hours a day.

Achimenes 'Charm'

SOIL AND NUTRIENTS

Use any fast-draining, sterilized soil mixture that is suitable for African violets. Add a tablespoon of sand or gravel to each pot to provide the calcium required by *Achimenes*. Fertilize plants once a month with fertilizer solution according to manufacturer's instructions. Do not use dried animal manure as fertilizer. It is too strong and will burn the tender, scaly rhizomes and roots.

WATER

It is essential to keep soil moderately moist. If soil dries out, the plant will go dormant prematurely, taking on a dry, dead appearance. Use water at room temperature. Be sure soil and pot drain properly.

HUMIDITY

Achimenes bloom from June to October and are dormant during late fall and winter months. Natural humidity in summer is generally sufficient. In extremely dry areas such as the American Southwest, daily misting around plants or placing plants on humidity trays may be beneficial. See Increasing Humidity, page 24.

TEMPERATURE

Normal summer temperatures in most areas of the United States and Canada are acceptable. Daytime temperatures of 75F (24C) or higher and nighttime temperatures of 65F to 70F (19C to 21C) are best. Temperatures required for winter storage are discussed under Dormancy, below.

PESTS AND DISEASES

Achimenes are usually free of pests and diseases, but are occasionally subject to the same problems as African violets. See Pests and Diseases, page 28.

DORMANCY

Plants bloom during summer and early fall. They are dormant during winter months. After bloom season has passed, leaves slowly turn brown and die. At this stage, stop watering plants. After leaves have withered, remove scaly rhizomes from plant. Pack them in plastic bags filled with dry vermiculite, perlite or peat moss. Rhizomes can also be left in pots for the winter. Store rhizomes through winter at around 60F (16C). In spring, pot with fresh soil.

PROPAGATION

Rooting stem cuttings, dividing roots or planting seeds are different ways to propagate *Achimenes*. See Propagation, page 35. The best way is to divide tiny, scaly rhizomes in fall when plant is dormant. Plant rhizomes in spring.

VARIETIES

Compact varieties are suitable for growing in pots. Intermediate-height varieties are best in pots or hanging baskets, because they are slightly pendulous. Grow taller varieties in pots. They become unmanageable in hanging baskets because of their rangy growth.

Achimenes 'Purple King'

Achimenes

Compact Plants—Suitable for Pots

NAME	BLOOM COLOR	BLOOM SIZE	LEAVES	GROWTH HABIT
'Ambroise Verschaffelt'	White face with purple veining	Medium	Medium green	Compact, less than 6 inches high
'Andrieuxi'	Violet and white	Medium	Medium green	Compact, about 8 inches high
'Atropurpurea'	Dark reddish purple with lilac throat	Medium	Medium green	Compact, about 8 inches high
'Camillo Brozzoni'	Purple with white throat	Small	Dark green	Compact, about 8 inches high
'Cettoana'	Blue tones	Medium	Dark green	Compact, about 10 inches high
'Charm'	Warm pink	Medium	Dark green	Compact, upright
'Francois Cardinaux'	Lavender and white	Medium	Medium green	Compact, profuse bloomer
'Violacea Semi-Plena'	Dark purple	Medium	Medium green	Compact, about 6 inches high

Intermediate Plants—Suitable for Pots or Hanging Baskets

NAME	BLOOM COLOR	BLOOM SIZE	LEAVES	GROWTH HABIT
'Adelaide'	Lavender with gold throat	Large	Dark green	Pendulous
'Cattleya'	Pastel orchid-blue	Medium	Medium green	Slightly pendulous
'Flava'	Golden yellow	Medium	Dark green	Somewhat rangy
'Grandiflora'	Purple with white throat	Medium	Medium green with red veins	Pendulous
'Heterophylla'	Bright orange	Medium	Dark green	Upright
'Mme. Geheune'	Reddish purple with red dots on throat	Large	Medium green	Pendulous
'Patens Major'	Purple	Small	Medium green	Slightly pendulous
'Pulchella'	Large, pale red	Medium	Medium green	Slightly pendulous
'Purple King'	Dark purple	Medium	Dark green	Slightly pendulous
'Vivid'	Magenta face with orange tube	Medium	Dark green	Slightly pendulous

Tall Plants—Suitable for Pots

NAME	BLOOM COLOR	BLOOM SIZE	LEAVES	GROWTH HABIT
'Antirrhina'	Vivid scarlet face with long, slender, yellow tubes	Medium	Medium green	Tall, slightly pendulous
'Lady Lyttelton'	Purple with gold throat	Medium	Medium green	Tall, slightly pendulous
'Master Ingram'	Long orange tubes with deep red	Medium	Medium green	Tall, slightly pendulous
'Pedunculata'	Fiery orange dots and lined with bright red	Medium	Medium green	Tallest *Achimenes*, slightly pendulous

Aeschynanthus
Lipstick vine, Basketvine

This popular gesneriad is native to Southeast Asia and the Himalayas. It is noted for its brilliant red, yellow and orange flower clusters. Tubelike clusters grow 1-1/2 to 4 inches long. Plants have a trailing growth habit. This makes them ideal for hanging baskets. Leaves are mottled and variegated in shades of green and red. *Aeschynanthus* usually bloom throughout the year. Branches grow 12 to 15 inches long. After blooming, cut back flowering branches to 6 inches.

Purchase plants from a nursery or mail-order house. Plants can also be started from seeds. See page 40.

LIGHT
Plants thrive with three or four hours of direct sunlight during winter. They should receive about 12 hours of bright, filtered light the rest of the year. A south or east window is the recommended exposure.

SOIL AND NUTRIENTS
An ideal soil mixture is 1 part potting soil, 1 part sharp sand or perlite and 2 parts peat moss or sphagnum moss. The large proportion of peat moss or sphagnum moss simulates soil conditions of a rain forest, their native habitat. Repotting is usually not necessary because plants thrive when potbound.

Fertilize once a month with a liquid African violet fertilizer according to manufacturer's instructions.

WATER
Aeschynanthus grow best in moist soil, so water frequently with room-temperature water. Be sure plant does not become waterlogged.

HUMIDITY
Plants do best with high humidity—50% or more. Misting around plants daily, particularly during winter, is recommended. See Increasing Humidity, page 24.

TEMPERATURE
Daytime temperatures of 75F (24C) or higher are recommended. Nighttime temperatures should be 65F to 70F (19C to 21C) during bloom. Temperatures of 55F to 60F (13C to 16C) help encourage bloom after dormancy.

PESTS AND DISEASES
Aeschynanthus are usually free from pests and diseases. If problems develop, see Pests and Diseases, page 28, for symptoms and solutions.

DORMANCY
Plants do not become dormant. Like most house plants, growth and bloom slow down during winter months.

PROPAGATION
Propagate from stem cuttings taken in spring. See Propagation, page 35.

Aeschynanthus 'Radicans'

Aeschynanthus 'Hildebrandtii'

Aeschynanthus

NAME	BLOOM COLOR	BLOOM SIZE	LEAVES	GROWTH HABIT
'Black Pagoda'	Dark red and yellow	Medium	Light and dark red and green variegated	Arching
'Ellipticus'	Light peach and salmon	Medium	Light green	Pendulous
'Hildebrandtii'	Scarlet	Medium	Medium green	Trailing
'Javanicus'	Red, orange, maroon and yellow	Medium to large	Dark green	Trailing and pendulous
'Kallimanton'	Dark red and yellow	Medium	Light and dark variegated red and green	Arching
'Lobbianus'	Red, orange, maroon and yellow	Medium to large	Dark green	Trailing and pendulous
'Marmoratus'	Green and maroon	Small to medium	Variegated red and green	Trailing
'Micranthus'	Dark red	Very small	Medium green	Pendulous, small plant
'Nummularius'	Dark red	Medium	Medium green	Small, arching, trailing
'Obconicus'	Dark red	Small	Dark green	Arching and trailing
'Parvifolius'	Red, orange, yellow and maroon	Medium	Red	Small, pendulous
'Pulcher'	Red and yellow	Medium to large	Light and dark green	Pendulous
'Radicans'	Red and yellow	Medium to large	Light green	Pendulous
'Speciosus'	Red, yellow and orange	Very large	Medium green	Arching, large plant
'Tricolor'	Red and yellow	Medium	Dark green	Pendulous, trailing
'X Splendidus'	Red, yellow and orange	Very large	Medium green	Arching, large plant

Columnea
Goldfish plant

The fibrous-rooted gesneriads called *Columnea* come from the rain forests of the West Indies and Central America. Flowers of *Columnea* resemble the tail of a fish; hence the common name, goldfish plant. Many varieties of this attractive plant have a trailing growth habit and are well suited for growing in hanging baskets. Some upright varieties are available. Foliage of most popular varieties is deep, waxy green or medium green. Leaves are elliptical or oval, from 1 to 6 inches long. Flowers are showy in red, yellow, orange and pink. They measure 1 to 3 inches long. Branches grow 12 to 15 inches long.

Purchase plants from a nursery or mail-order house. You can also grow them from seeds or propagate them in other ways. See Propagation, page 35.

LIGHT
Columneas have the same general light requirements as African violets. During winter, place plants in an east window or shaded south window. During summer, plants thrive on a shaded porch or hanging beneath a tree. Plants can also be grown under artificial light but are not well suited because of their large size. If artificial light is used, give plants about 12 to 14 hours of light a day. Keep plants 6 to 10 inches away from light tubes.

SOIL AND NUTRIENTS
Plant in light, well-drained soil such as commercial African violet soil. Soilless mixes are also satisfactory. The Nassau County Extension Service in New York recommends a mix of equal parts perlite, vermiculite and shredded peat moss. For every bushel of mix, add 1/2 pound limestone and 1/2 pound of time-release fertilizer. Time-release fertilizers usually last 6 months. If soil compacts, add sphagnum moss, perlite or small pieces of styrofoam cups to aid drainage.

WATER
Water thoroughly with room-temperature water. Allow soil surface to dry completely before watering again. Signs of insufficient watering are dropping of small leaves and curling of larger leaves. If this happens, submerge the pot about halfway in a pan filled with room-temperature water.

Overwatering or erratic watering may cause *stem rot,* also called *petiole rot,* a disease that causes stems to shrivel and older leaves to drop. If stem rot occurs, water sparingly but regularly. Treat plant with a fungicide such as benomyl. See Pests and Diseases, page 32. If stem rot persists, take cuttings of *healthy* stems from infected plant and start new plants.

HUMIDITY
Columneas require at least 50% humidity to thrive. Humidity levels should be in direct proportion to temperature. The higher the temperature, the higher the humidity. For example, at 70F (21C), 50% humidity is recommended. At 80F (27C), 60% humidity is recommended. See Increasing Humidity, page 24.

Columnea 'Cardinal'

TEMPERATURE
Plants are more tolerant of cold than most gesneriads, but should not be exposed to temperatures below 55F (13C). At 45F (7C), plants are severely damaged. Leaves turn brown and drop.

Ideal daytime temperatures are 65F to 75F (19C to 24C). If temperatures go above 80F (27C), plants may suffer. A nighttime drop of 5 to 10 degrees from the daytime temperature is beneficial to plants.

PESTS AND DISEASES
Columneas are resistant to most pests and diseases. Aphids, cyclamen mites and whiteflies are occasional problems.

DORMANCY
Plants do not go into dormancy. Growth slows down and plants rest during winter months.

PROPAGATION
Take stem cuttings any time of the year. Cuttings should be 3 to 4 inches long. Remove leaves from lower one-third of each cutting. Insert a cutting in each pot filled with moist, planting medium such as equal amounts of perlite and vermiculite. Enclose cutting and pot in a plastic bag and place out of direct sunlight. After cuttings have rooted, plant three or four in a pot, setting them near the pot's center.

Columnea 'Oneidan'

Columnea 'Yellow Bird'

Columnea

NAME	BLOOM COLOR	BLOOM SIZE	LEAVES	GROWTH HABIT
'Arguta'	Orange-red flowers bloom in fall	Large	Small, dark green	Pendulous
'Bonfire'	Everblooming orange-red flowers	Large	Small, light green	Arching, bushy
'Campus Gem'	Red flowers bloom winter and spring	Medium to large	Small, light green	Trailing, bushy
'Campus Queen'	Everblooming purple flowers	Small	Small, narrow dark green	Bushy
'Campus Sunset'	Everblooming red, orange and yellow flowers	Medium to large	Medium-size, dark red	Trailing
'Canary'	Everblooming yellow flowers	Small to medium	Small, dark red	Bushy
'Cardinal'	Everblooming red flowers	Medium to large	Medium-size, dark green	Trailing
'Cascadilla'	Everblooming red-orange flowers	Large	Medium-size, dark green	Trailing
'Cayugan'	Orange flowers bloom winter and spring	Medium	Narrow, medium green	Trailing
'Chocolate Soldier'	Sometimes everblooming red flowers	Large	Small, dark red	Arching
'Early Bird'	Everblooming orange to reddish-yellow flowers	Medium	Small, medium green	Pendulous, trailing
'Erythropaea'	Everblooming orange to reddish-yellow flowers	Large	Medium-size, dark green	Arching
'Fanfare'	Everblooming orange-yellow flowers	Small	Small, dark green	Pendulous, trailing
'Fang'	Everblooming orange-yellow flowers	Medium	Small, dark green	Pendulous, trailing

NAME	BLOOM COLOR	BLOOM SIZE	LEAVES	GROWTH HABIT
'Gloriosa Superba'	Red-yellow flowers bloom fall, winter and spring	Large	Small, dark red	Pendulous
'Gold Spice'	Everblooming orange-yellow flowers	Large	Medium-size, dark red	Trailing
'Hirta'	Orange flowers bloom winter and spring	Large	Small, narrow, medium green	Bushy, trailing
'Ithacan'	Everblooming red-orange	Large flowers	Medium-size, dark red	Arching, trailing
'Joy'	Everblooming red to orange-yellow flowers	Medium	Small, medium green	Pendulous, trailing
'Lepidocaula'	Everblooming orange flowers	Large	Medium-size, dark green	Bushy, upright
'Linearis'	Everblooming purple flowers	Small	Narrow, small, medium green	Bushy, upright
'Mia'	Everblooming red-orange flowers	Medium to large	Small, medium green	Pendulous
'Microphylla'	Red flowers bloom in spring	Medium	Tiny, medium green	Trailing, pendulous
'Moon Glow'	Everblooming yellow flowers with red hairs	Large	Medium-size red	Trailing
'Mooreii Var'	Red flowers bloom winter and spring	Medium	Tiny, variegated	Bushy, trailing
'Oneidan'	Orange-red flowers bloom winter and spring	Large	Small, dark green	Arching
'Onondagan'	Everblooming red flowers	Large	Medium-size, dark red	Arching, trailing
'Orange Princess'	Yellow to orange-red flowers	Large	Medium-size, red	Arching
'Orange Queen'	Orange flowers bloom winter and spring	Large	Medium-size, light green	Arching
'Orange Zing'	Everblooming orange to red-yellow flowers	Large	Small, red	Pendulous
'Othello'	Everblooming red flowers	Large	Medium-size, dark red	Arching, trailing
'Percrassa'	Everblooming red flowers	Small	Small, medium green	Bushy, arching
'Pilosissima'	Everblooming orange-red flowers	Medium	Small, light green	Arching, trailing
'Red Spur'	Everblooming red-yellow flowers	Large	Small, dark red	Trailing
'Robin'	Everblooming dark-red flowers	Large	Medium-size, dark red	Trailing
'Stavenger'	Red flowers bloom in spring, but require cool conditions	Medium	Small, medium green	Arching, trailing
'Teusherii minor'	Purple, red or yellow flowers bloom in spring	Medium	Medium-size, medium green	Pendulous
'Tiogan'	Purple-orange flowers bloom winter and spring	Large	Small, narrow, medium green	Bushy, trailing
'Wonder'	Everblooming red-orange flowers	Large	Medium-size, dark red	Arching
'Yellow Bird'	Everblooming yellow flowers	Large	Medium-size, dark red	Trailing
'Yellow Dragon'	Everblooming yellow-orange flowers	Large	Medium-size, dark red	Trailing

Episcia
Flame Violet, Peacock Plant

Episcia, pronounced *Ee-pish-ee-a* or *Ee-piss-ee-a,* include some of the most spectacular gesneriads. The most popular and available varieties produce brillant red, scarlet or orange flowers. Leaves have a slight, pebbly texture that resembles luxurious silk brocades, quilts or tapestries. Leaves are colored various shades of green, burgundy, chocolate and copper with silver or white veins. Some have pink and white albino leaves. Their *stolons,* slender branches or shoots that develop a bud and root at the tip, make them suitable for hanging baskets. Plants grow to 10 inches high, with branches trailing to 12 inches. Most are native to Central and South America.

Episcias are usually purchased directly from a nursery or mail-order supplier. Plants can be grown from seeds and propagated in other ways. See Propagation, page 35.

LIGHT
Generally, *Episcias* prefer more light than African violets. If you want to grow them for foliage only, a north window will do. If you want to enjoy the beautiful flowers, place them in an eastern window or partially shaded southern window.

Plants grown under fluorescent light need 14 to 16 hours of light each day. Keep light tubes 4 to 6 inches away from top of plant.

If leaves begin to lose their color, move plants to a window with less light. Or place them a greater distance from the fluorescent light.

SOIL AND NUTRIENTS
Plant in a porous, well-drained, African violet mixture. Plants also thrive in non-organic materials such as perlite, vermiculite or gravel. Feed plants grown in a soil mix two times a month with a liquid fertilizer. Feed plants grown in non-organic materials with quarter-strength fertilizer solution with each watering. See Fertilizer, page 26.

WATER
Episcias prefer wetter conditions than African violets and most other gesneriads. Use room-temperature water and keep soil moist at all times. Good drainage is essential. Don't allow pots to "stand" in water. If water is splashed on foliage, remove plants from direct sunlight until water has evaporated, or leaves will burn.

Episcia 'Faded Jade'

HUMIDITY

Humidity must be maintained between 45% and 75% to have prolific bloom. Place plants on humidity trays filled with water. Place pebbles in tray to hold bottom of pot above water level. As the water evaporates, humidity around plants increases. Other ways to increase humidity are discussed on page 24.

TEMPERATURE

Episcias thrive in temperatures ranging from 75F to 80F (24C to 27C) during the day, with a slight drop at night. Plants are damaged at 60F (16C). They may die below 55F (13C). Keep plants out of drafts.

PESTS AND DISEASES

Plants are subject to the same pests and diseases that attack other gesneriads. See Pests and Diseases, page 28, for identification and solutions to plant problems.

DORMANCY

Episcias do not go into dormancy, but growth slows and plants rest during winter months.

PROPAGATION

Propagate from stolons, leaf cuttings and seeds.

Stolons—This is the quickest and most successful method. Stolons are slender branches or shoots that develop a bud and root at the tip. They are located at the terminals of branches or lateral shoots. Cut stolon from mother plant and treat cut end with rooting hormone powder. Insert in perlite, vermiculite, sand or sphagnum peat moss. Or place stolon in a glass of water away from direct sunlight. See pages 37 and 38.

Leaves—Leaves are slower to root and less successful compared to stolons. Select medium-size leaf from healthy plant. Using sterilized scissors or razor, remove 1-1/2 to 2 inches of stem along with leaf. Dip end of stem in rooting hormone powder and insert in pot filled with planting medium. Cover pot and leaf with a plastic bag or water glass. This increases humidity and helps speed rooting.

Seeds—Place potting soil, peat moss or vermiculite in a pot. Sprinkle the tiny seeds over the medium. Place pot in warm water until surface of medium becomes wet. Cover with plastic and set in bright light, out of direct sun. Seeds should germinate in 1 to 2 weeks. Place seedlings under fluorescent light, about 3 inches from tube. Or place in an east window. When seedlings are about 1 inch high, transplant each to individual pots.

Episcia 'Triton'

Episcia

NAME	BLOOM COLOR	BLOOM SIZE	LEAVES	GROWTH HABIT
'Acajou'	Red	Medium	Large, dark green and silver variegated	Low growing
'Cameo'	Orange-red	Medium	Medium-size, dark green, purple, red and silver variegated	Low growing
'Canal Zone Hybrid'	Red-orange	Medium	Medium-size, light and dark variegated	Low growing
'Chocolate Soldier'	Red	Medium	Large, dark chocolate-green and silver variegated	Low growing
'Columbia Orange'	Orange	Medium	Large, light green	Low growing
'Coral Glow'	Red	Medium	Medium-size, dark pink and red	Low growing
'Dianthaflora'	White	Medium	Small, medium green	Low growing
'Elizabeth'	Red	Medium	Large, light and dark, silver and green variegated	Low growing
'Ember Lace'	Pink	Medium	Medium-size, light and dark green and pink variegated	Low growing
'Faded Jade'	Red	Medium	Medium-size, light silver and green variegated	Low growing
'Filigree'	Red-orange	Medium	Medium-size, light and dark green and silver variegated	Low growing
'Fire 'n' Ice'	Red	Medium	Large, light silver and green variegated	Low growing
'Flamingo'	Red	Medium	Large pink	Low growing
'Green Haga'	Pink	Medium	Medium-size, light and dark silver and green variegated	Low growing
'Lilacina'	Lilac	Medium	Medium-size, light silver and green variegated	Low growing
'Moss Agate'	Red	Medium	Large, silver variegated	Low growing
'Mrs. Fanny Haage'	Lilac	Medium	Medium-size, light and dark silver and green variegated	Low growing
'Noel'	Red	Medium	Large, light green	Low growing
'Painted Warrior'	Pink, red and orange	Medium	Medium-size, dark and light pink and green variegated	Low growing
'Persian Carpet'	Red	Medium	Large, dark green and silver variegated	Low growing
'Pink Brocade'	Red-orange	Medium	Medium-size, dark and light silver and green variegated	Low growing
'Pinkiscia'	Red	Medium	Medium-size, dark and light silver and green variegated	Low growing
'Reptans Bronze Queen'	Red	Medium	Large, dark green and silver variegated	Low growing
'Ruby'	Red-orange	Medium	Medium-size, light and dark red and green variegated	Low growing
'Shimmer'	Red	Medium	Large, light and dark silver and green variegated	Low growing
'Silver Sheen'	Red	Medium	Large, light and dark silver and green variegated	Low growing
'Tricolor'	Red	Medium	Medium-size, dark and light green and silver variegated .	Low growing
'Triton'	Red	Medium	Medium-size, dark green and silver variegated	Low growing
'Tropical Topaz'	Yellow	Medium	Medium-size, light green	Low growing
'Velvet Princess'	Red	Medium	Medium-size, light green and silver variegated	Low growing

Kohleria

There are more than 50 species of *Kohleria,* but only a few are grown by hobbyists. All have an upright growth habit except 'Amabilis', which has a trailing habit, suitable for hanging-basket culture.

Kohleria originated in tropical areas of the Western Hemisphere. Flowers have five petals, are tuberous and come in several bright colors, often spotted with other colors. Leaves are hairy and often mottled. Plants grow 8 to 16 inches high.

Kohleria is grown from scaly rhizomes, similar to *Achimenes,* but rhizomes are longer. *Rhizomes* are rootlike stems that send up leafy shoots from the upper surface and roots from the lower surface.

The *rest period,* when plant is dormant, is considerably shorter than for *Achimenes.* Plant can be made to bloom any time of the year. After bloom, cut back flowering branches to soil level. New growth will produce more flowers.

Buy plants from nurseries or mail-order sources. You can also purchase rhizomes and plant the same as *Achimenes.* See page 114.

LIGHT
As with most gesneriads, filtered sunlight is best. Partially shaded south or east windows are recommended. If plants are grown under fluorescent light, provide with 14 to 16 hours of light a day.

SOIL AND NUTRIENTS
Plant in any commercially available African violet soil mixture. Fertilize once a month with African violet fertilizer according to instructions on product label.

WATER
Keep moist with room-temperature water and provide good drainage.

HUMIDITY
Use trays filled with pebbles to increase humidity. Mist around plants frequently during winter months while house is being heated. Humidity during summer is generally sufficient. See Increasing Humidity, page 24.

TEMPERATURE
Temperatures of 75F (24C) or higher are ideal during daytime. Maintain nighttime temperatures at 65F to 70F (19C to 21C).

PESTS AND DISEASES
Kohlerias are generally free from pests and diseases. If problems develop, see Pests and Diseases, page 28, for identification and treatment.

DORMANCY
Plants have a short dormancy period, normally lasting from two to three months. Growth pattern is similar to *Achimenes.*

PROPAGATION
Make stem cuttings of new growth. Or divide scaly rhizomes during semidormant stage. See *Achimenes,* page 115, for instructions.

Kohleria 'Bella'

Kohleria 'Rongo'

Kohleria

NAME	BLOOM COLOR	BLOOM SIZE	LEAVES	GROWTH HABIT
'Amabilis'	Dark red-orange spots, red-orange tube	Medium	Mottled light and dark green	Pendulous
'Bella'	Yellow with red spots, pink and red tube	Medium	Medium green	Upright
'Carnival'	Yellow with red spots, red tube	Medium	Medium green	Upright
'Connecticut Belle'	Pink with magenta spots, rose-red tube	Medium	Mottled light green with dark-red underside	Upright
'Eriantha'	Yellow and red with red and magenta spots, orange-red tube	Medium	Bright green with rust edge	Upright
'Longwood'	Red with dark red spots, red tube	Medium	Medium green with dark-red underside	Upright
'Platylomata'	Red with yellow spots, red tube	Medium	Variegated shades of green, silver with red underside	Upright, bushy
'Princess'	Pink with fuchsia spots, pink tube	Medium	Mottled light green with red underside	Upright
'Rongo'	Pinkish white with magenta spots, rose tube	Medium	Medium green	Upright

Nematanthus
Threadflower

This cousin of *Columnea* is native to Brazil. The pouch-shape flowers come in various shades of orange, red, pink and yellow. They bloom amid handsome, glossy green foliage. Recently, the American Gloxinia and Gesneriad Society included most of the species formerly listed with *Hypocyrta* into this genus.

Nematanthus are particularly suited for growing in hanging baskets. Plants grow to 10 inches high, with trailing branches to 2 or more feet long.

Growth requirements are identical to those of *Columnea*. See page 119 for instructions. Some varieties bloom all year under ideal conditions. Some tend to have a late-summer dormant period, and leaves fall from the plant. No everblooming varieties are available. Interest in hybridizing this species may create everblooming plants.

Like *Columnea, Nematanthus* are usually purchased as plants from nurseries or mail-order sources. You can also grow plants from seeds, or propagate from plant parts. See Propagation, page 35.

DORMANCY
Nematanthus does not go into dormancy. Growth and bloom slow during winter months.

Nematanthus 'Jungle Lights'

Nematanthus

NAME	BLOOM COLOR	BLOOM SIZE	LEAVES	GROWTH HABIT
'Bambino'	Orange and red	Small	Small, glossy, dark green with red marks on underside	Very dwarf
'Black Gold'	Gold	Medium	Dark green	Bushy
'Black Magic'	Red to orange-yellow	Medium	Small, glossy, dark green with red underside	Bushy, slightly droopy
'Butterscotch'	Yellow	Medium	Satiny, bronze-green	Bushy
'Cheerio'	Orange-yellow	Medium	Small, waxy, shiny, dark green	Bushy
'Christmas Holly'	Bright red	Medium	Small, shiny green	Bushy
'Encore'	Yellow-tipped orange	Medium	Small, glossy, dark green	Compact, semitrailing
'Fritschii'	Pink	Large	Large, dark green and red variegated	Arching, spreading
'Green Magic'	Red to orange-yellow	Large	Small, glossy, light green	Bushy, slightly droopy
'Gregarius'	Orange	Medium	Glossy, dark green	Bushy, slightly droopy
'Jungle Lights'	Orange-yellow	Medium	Glossy, dark green	Arching, spreading
'Longipes'	Red	Large	Large, shiny, light green	Arching, spreading
'Nervosus'	Red-orange	Medium	Small, dark green	Bushy, slightly droopy
'Perianthomegus'	Yellow	Large	Large, glossy, light green	Bushy, upright
'Rio'	Red to orange-yellow	Medium	Small, glossy, light green	Bushy
'Stoplight'	Rosy red	Medium	Large, red and green variegated	Arching, spreading
'Strigillosus'	Red	Medium	Small, medium green	Bushy, slightly droopy
'Tropicana'	Red-yellow	Large	Small, glossy, dark green and red	Bushy, slightly droopy
'Wettsteinii'	Orange-yellow	Medium	Tiny, shiny, dark green and red	Bushy, slightly droopy

Gloxinia 'Emperor Frederick' type

Sinningia

Gloxinia, Slipper plant

There are three major species of *Sinningia* grown by hobbyists. All are natives of Brazil. Most popular is *Sinningia speciosa,* commonly called *gloxinia.* These beautiful flowers are known almost universally by that name. Familiar to many house-plant gardeners, this handsome plant sports large, inverted, bell-shape flowers. Colors are red, purple, blue, pink and white and combinations. Flowers can be single or double. They grow on strong stems above a rosette of large, velvety, hairy, medium-green leaves.

Plants grow 12 to 14 inches high when in bloom. They require a period of dormancy after bloom. You can purchase mature plants from most florists, or tubers or seeds from mail-order sources. You can also propagate from leaves or cuttings.

MINIATURE SINNINGIA
Culture for standard and miniature varieties of *Sinningia* is the same as for gloxinia. If you plant them in a terrarium or brandy snifter, they grow much more vigorously than in pots. In addition, the miniatures are everblooming if you water them regularly throughout the year. If you cease to water, plants will go into dormancy like their larger sisters and gloxinia cousins.

With all types of *Sinningias,* purchase *tubers*—fleshy underground stems—from nursery or mail-order source. Plant tubers in a 6-inch tub as soon as they are purchased. A *tub* differs from a *pot* in that it is 3/4 as tall as it is wide. Place tuber, inverted side facing up, in the tub. Cover with about 1/2 inch of African violet soil mixture. Water thoroughly after planting. Water sparingly thereafter until plant starts its growth cycle.

LIGHT
Gloxinias require long exposure to strong light. Place in a south or east window. In spring, fall and winter, expose plant to full sun. Filter sunlight only during summer. If grown under fluorescent light, provide plants with 14 to 16 hours a day.

SOIL AND NUTRIENTS
Any African violet soil mixture is acceptable. Feed monthly with liquid African violet fertilizer according to manufacturer's instructions. After plant completes its bloom cycle and goes dormant, allow plant to rest. When new growth commences, remove tuber from pot and plant in fresh soil.

WATER
Keep soil barely moist during growing season. Don't overwater, or plant may suffer from crown rot. During dormant stage, water only enough to keep tuber from shriveling and drying out. When soil becomes distinctly dry, water lightly. As a guide, watering should be necessary only three or four times during the dormant period.

Sinningia 'Sylvatica'

HUMIDITY

Gloxinias require high humidity. If humidity is too low, leaves will dry out and buds will fall off. Daily misting around, but not directly on, plant foliage helps somewhat. Humidity trays and humidifiers can also be used.

TEMPERATURE

Daytime temperatures of 75F (24C) or higher are recommended. Nighttime temperatures of 65F to 70F (19C to 21C) are best. If temperature falls below 60F (16C), plant will not bloom and grow to its potential.

PESTS AND DISEASES

Gloxinias have few problems with pests and diseases. Occasionally black-leg disease becomes a problem. If leaves and stems turn black, isolate plant. Remove all foliage and soak tubers with solution of benlate, a fungicide. Tubers usually resprout.

DORMANCY

After plants have bloomed and no new buds or flowers can be seen, withhold water until leaves become yellow and wither. Allow leaves to turn brown and die. Remove dead foliage and store tub with tuber in soil in a warm cellar or closet. Leave in storage for 6 to 10 weeks. This gives the tuber a *rest period*. During this time, water only enough to keep tuber from shriveling and drying out. When new growth appears, remove tuber, pot in new soil and begin watering sparingly. As growth increases, provide more water.

PROPAGATION

Gloxinias can be propagated from seeds, sprouts from tubers and leaf cuttings. In addition, you can propagate using the *rib* of a healthy leaf. This is the main axis running up the center of the leaf. Remove healthy stem and leaf from plant. Cut part way through rib in several places, cutting perpendicular to its length. Place stem end of leaf in planting medium and the leaf itself on the medium. Press leaf so that rib and cuts are in contact with medium. Cover with glass or plastic until roots form. Small tubers will develop at each cut.

Standard Sinningia

NAME	BLOOM COLOR	BLOOM SIZE	LEAVES	GROWTH HABIT
'Aggregata'	Red	Very small	Soft, medium green	Tall, 1 foot or more with tendency to droop. The only member of the gesneriad family that has a pleasant fragrance
'Barbata'	White	Small	Small, glossy, dark blue-green with red undersides	Shrubby and upright
'Canescens'	Brilliant scarlet, singly or in clusters	Medium	Light green to silver, woolly texture	Upright, to about 12 inches across
'Coral Belle'	Coral with purple-veined throat	Small	Various shades of green	Compact, small
'Eumorpha'	White or light-lavender flush	Medium	Glossy green	Rosette with short stems
'Hirsuta'	White with dark purple	Medium	Medium green	Rosette
'Laurie'	Pure white with yellow stripe in throat	Medium	Medium green	Upright
'Melinda'	Pale lavender with red hairs, purple veins	Medium	Medium green	Upright
'Pendulina'	Bright orange-red	Small	Soft, flexible, medium green	Small, bushy growth
'Regina' ('Brazilian Gloxinia')	Violet	Small	Dark green, veined white with red underside	Short stems
'Sylvatica'	Orange-red	Medium	Light green, woolly texture	Spreading, low grower
'Tubiflora'	White	Medium	Medium green	Tall

Gloxinia 'Trudy' type

Gloxinia 'B26' type

Gloxinia 'Etoile De Feu' type

Gloxinia

Named Varieties

Hundreds of varieties of gloxinia are available. Some are named; some are named only as numbers. Many are unnamed and sold by color. These are the most readily available named varieties.

NAME	BLOOM COLOR	BLOOM SIZE	LEAVES	GROWTH HABIT
'Crispa Meteor'	Scarlet, ruffled and fringed	Large	Medium green	Spreading, low grower
'Emperor Frederick'	Scarlet with white border	Large	Medium green	Spreading, low grower
'Emperor Wilhelm'	Blue with white border	Large	Medium green	Spreading, low grower
'Etoile De Feu'	Rich scarlet	Large	Medium green	Spreading, low grower
'Gigantea Red Tigrina'	White speckled with bright red	Large	Medium green	Spreading, low grower
'Hollywood'	Soft violet	Large	Medium green	Spreading, low grower
'Kegeljani White'	Pure white	Large	Medium green	Spreading, low grower
'Prince Albert'	Dark blue with frilled edge	Large	Medium green	Spreading, low grower
'Queen Wilhelmina'	Pink with violet sheen	Large	Medium green	Spreading, low grower
'Trudy'	Dark pink with white throat	Large	Medium green	Spreading, low grower
'Violacea'	Soft violet	Large	Medium green	Spreading, low grower
'Waterloo'	Dark red with ruffled and fringed edge	Large	Medium green	Spreading, low grower

Gloxinia 'B24' type

Gloxinia

Numbered Varieties

Many unusual varieties are available by mail order from Buell's Greenhouses, Inc., Box 218, Eastford, CT 06242. Buell's is a major hybridizer of gloxinias in the United States. Their varieties are not named but numbered. This is a sample of their varieties.

NAME	BLOOM COLOR	BLOOM SIZE	LEAVES	GROWTH HABIT
'B1'	Shades of dark purple	Large	Medium green	Spreading, low grower
'B2'	Light purple-blue with white or light throat	Large	Medium green	Spreading, low grower
'B3'	Dark purple border with speckled throat	Large	Medium green	Spreading, low grower
'B10'	Pink to rose-pink, heavily speckled throughout with darker pink border	Large	Medium green	Spreading, low grower
'B12'	Red, white and blue	Large	Medium green	Spreading, low grower
'B15'	Various shades of plum	Large	Medium green	Spreading, low grower
'B20'	White with light to deep pink border	Large	Medium green	Spreading, low grower
'B22'	White with purple or blue speckles	Large	Medium green	Spreading, low grower
'B24'	White tinted with pink to red	Large	Medium green	Spreading, low grower
'B26'	Purple with white border	Large	Medium green	Spreading, low grower

Smithiantha
Temple bells

Smithianthas are native to Mexico, and closely related to *Achimenes* and *Kohleria*. They also grow from scaly rhizomes. Flowers are funnel shape with small lobes. They are borne on spikes that grow from the center of the plant. Colors are white, pink, red, orange or yellow, streaked or blotched with contrasting shades. Foliage is handsome, usually deep green and heart shape, often mottled with red, purple and bronze. Flowers bloom from late summer into winter. Following bloom, they go into dormancy like *Achimenes*.

Plants grow 8 to 12 inches high, with flower stems reaching to 2 feet. A group called *Cornell hybrids* grow to 2 feet tall. These are not recommended for window-sill cultivation. They are better suited to greenhouse culture. The miniature hybrids listed below are best grown indoors.

Smithianthas are usually purchased as plants from a nursery or mail-order source. They can also be grown from seeds or propagated by other methods.

LIGHT
As with *Achimenes* and other gesneriads, filtered sunlight is recommended. If plants are grown under fluorescent light, provide 14 to 16 hours of light each day.

SOIL AND NUTRIENTS
Any African violet soil mixture is appropriate. Feed once a month during growing season with a liquid African violet fertilizer according to manufacturer's instructions.

WATER
Provide proper drainage and water moderately with room-temperature water during the growing season—April to October. After bloom, when plants wither and become dormant, water lightly to keep rhizomes from drying out. Avoid wetting leaves as much as possible.

HUMIDITY
During growing season, natural humidity should be sufficient for healthy growth. During winter when your home is heated, increase humidity while plants are still growing before they become dormant. Increase humidity again after new growth commences. See Increasing Humidity, page 24. Keep *Smithianthas* out of drafts.

TEMPERATURE
Daytime temperatures of 75F (24C) or higher are recommended. Nighttime temperatures of 65F to 70F (19C to 21C) are ideal.

PESTS AND DISEASES
Smithianthas are reasonably pest- and disease-free. Should problems arise, see Pests and Diseases, page 28.

DORMANCY
See *Achimenes,* Dormancy, page 115, for instructions.

PROPAGATION
Propagate from stem cuttings. Take cuttings any time during the growing season. Or divide rhizomes during dormancy. See Propagation, page 35.

Cornell Smithiantha Hybrids

Two general types of *Smithiantha* are available. *Cornell* hybrids grow to 2 feet tall. *Miniature* hybrids are more compact and grow to about 1 foot high.

NAME	BLOOM COLOR	BLOOM SIZE	LEAVES	GROWTH HABIT
'Abbey'	Peach	Medium	Plain	Tall, upright
'Capistrano'	Red	Medium	Mottled	Tall, upright
'Carmel'	Red-orange	Medium	Mottled	Tall, upright
'Cathedral'	Yellow-orange	Medium	Plain	Tall, upright
'Matins'	Red	Medium	Plain	Tall, upright
'San Gabriel'	Orange	Medium	Mottled	Tall, upright
'Santa Barbara'	Yellow-orange	Medium	Mottled	Tall, upright
'Santa Clara'	Peach-orange	Medium	Mottled	Tall, upright
'Vespers'	Orange-red	Medium	Plain	Tall, upright

Miniature Smithiantha

NAME	BLOOM COLOR	BLOOM SIZE	LEAVES	GROWTH HABIT
'Little Tudor'	Orange to red-yellow	Very small	Red and purple mottled	Compact
'Little Wonder'	Rose-yellow	Very small	Red mottled	Compact
'Little Yellow'	Yellow and red	Very small	Plain	Compact

Smithiantha species

Streptocarpus
Cape primrose

The popularity of *Streptocarpus* is increasing among gesneriad hobbyists. The common name, cape primrose, stems from its origin, the Cape of Good Hope in Africa. Foliage also resembles that of the perennial garden primrose. Plants grow to 15 inches high. They can bloom any time of the year, producing 2- to 5-inch, trumpet-shape flowers in white, pink, rose, red, blue and purple. Many varieties have fringed edges and throats with different colorations. Foliage is narrow, usually medium green and hairy with a quilted texture. Leaves are stemless, growing much like the popular garden primrose. *Streptocarpus* is at its prime during the second and subsequent years.

After flowering, cut back blossom stems to just above soil level. This way the energy of the plant does not go into producing seeds.

Purchase plants from a nursery or mail-order source. You can also grow plants from seeds or propagate in a variety of ways. For step-by-step instructions, see Propagation, page 35.

LIGHT
Like most gesneriads, *Streptocarpus* require several hours of indirect light. A south or east window with sunlight filtering through curtains is ideal. Provide 14 to 16 hours a day if grown under fluorescent light.

SOIL AND NUTRIENTS
Any African violet soil mix is acceptable. Fertilize with liquid African violet fertilizer once a month according to the product label.

WATER
Keep soil evenly moist with room-temperature water. *Streptocarpus saxorum* does not go into dormancy after bloom, so water regularly throughout the year. *Streptocarpus rexii* rests after bloom, so water sparingly at this time—just enough so leaves do not wilt.

HUMIDITY
Moderate humidity—50% to 60%—is required. Humidity during summer is usually sufficient. During the winter heating season, place plants on a humidity tray to help increase humidity level. Do not spray water on leaves.

TEMPERATURE
During the day, temperatures of 75F (24C) or higher are recommended. During the night, temperatures of 60F to 70F (16C to 21C) are ideal.

PESTS AND DISEASES
Whiteflies, thrips and red spider mites occasionally attack plants. See Pests and Diseases, page 30.

DORMANCY
Streptocarpus does not go into dormancy. After bloom, cut back flower stems.

PROPAGATION
Grow from seeds or propagate from division or stem cuttings. Leaf cuttings may be propagated by removing a leaf and laying it on the surface of a planting medium. Or remove leaf and cut it lengthwise along the center vein. Insert the cut edges of the sections into soil. Prevent drying out by covering cuttings and planting medium with plastic or glass.

Streptocarpus 'Holst II'

Streptocarpus

Bavarian Belle Rexii Hybrids

NAME	BLOOM COLOR	BLOOM SIZE	LEAVES	GROWTH HABIT
'Freda'	Rich red with white throat	Large	Narrow, medium green, hairy, quilted	Clumplike growth
'Ilsa'	White with purple markings	Large	Narrow, medium green, hairy, quilted	Clumplike growth
'Marta'	Dark purple with yellow throat	Large	Narrow, medium green, hairy, quilted	Clumplike growth
'Velma'	Rose with white throat	Large	Narrow, medium green, hairy, quilted	Clumplike growth

Other Varieties

Rexii hybrids other than the Bavarian Belle series are stemless and have long, straplike, quilted, medium-green leaves. They are everblooming with 2- to 3-inch-long trumpet-shape flowers on tall stems. Colors range from white to deep pink, purple and red. Many are striped.

NAME	BLOOM COLOR	BLOOM SIZE	LEAVES	GROWTH HABIT
'Blue Lace'	Lavender-blue and white	Large	Medium-size, medium green, hairy, quilted	Clumplike growth
'Gardenii'	Pale lavender with deep-violet lines	Large	Narrow, medium green, hairy, quilted	Clumplike growth
'Good Hope'	Bright lavender-blue	Large	Narrow, medium green, hairy, quilted	Clumplike growth
'Holst II'	Bright blue	Large	Narrow, medium green, hairy, quilted	Clumplike growth
'Kirkii'	Delicate lavender-blue	Large	Narrow, medium green, hairy, quilted	Clumplike growth
'Saxorum'	Light lavender-blue	Large	Long, hairy, medium green	Leaves drape nicely from hanging baskets

Streptocarpus 'Blue Lace'

Lesser-Known Gesneriads

Hundreds of other gesneriads can be grown as house plants. Of these, only a few are available. Many of the plants listed in this section cannot be purchased at your local nursery or florist. If you are interested in growing any of these plants, join the American Gloxinia and Gesneriad Society, P. O. Box 312, Ayer, MA 01432. You should be able to acquire seeds, leaf cuttings or plants from members of the Society.

Agalmyla
This genus comes from Asia and is similar to *Aeschynanthus.* Red flowers are borne in large clusters in the leaf axils on stems.

Alloplectus
Cylindrical flowers are red or yellow with contrasting colors in the throat. Foliage is trailing with velvety, dull-green leaves. Plant adapts nicely to hanging baskets. Native to Central America.

Asteranthera
This plant bears raspberry-red flowers and has small, oval leaves. It can be grown outdoors in mild-winter areas. A native of Chile.

Bellonia
Small leaves and arching, woody stems characterize this plant. Flowers are white. *Bellonia spinosa* is the only gesneriad with thorns. Native to the West Indies.

Besleria
Flowers are white, yellow, orange or red. Plants have fibrous roots. *Besleria maasii* is compact and erect. Adapts to being grown indoors. Native to Central and South America and the West Indies.

Briggsia
Flowers are yellow, sometimes with red spots. *Briggsia muscicola* is the best known. This semihardy alpine is native to the Himalayas and China.

Chirita
Flowers are lavender with silver and green marbled leaves. Plants thrive in moderate temperatures, 70F to 80F (21C to 27C). Supply with high humidity and light shade. Native to southeast Asia.

Codonanthe
Codonanthe species grow upright to about 18 inches high. Flowers of *C. crassifolia* and *C. macradenia* have white petals with pink or yellow throats. Lower leaves have red dots. *C. luteola* has pastel-yellow blooms. Smaller species, mostly with white flowers, include *C. digna* and *C. carnosa.* Both are easy to grow. All are tuberous-rooted natives of the South-American tropics.

Gesneria
The smaller species of this large genera are suited for indoor culture. *Gesneria cuneifolia* has shiny, medium-green leaves and bright-red flowers that resemble firecrackers. Other red-flowering varieties include *G. acaulis, G. christii* and *G. pedicellaris. G. citrina* has yellow flowers. *G. pumila* has white flowers. *G. pauciflora* has orange flowers.

Koellikeria
This is a small plant that adapts well to terrarium culture. It grows from scaly rhizomes like *Achimenes.* Flowers are white with deep-red markings. Leaves grow in rosettes about 2 to 4 inches across. Native to Central and South America.

Nautilocalyx
Nautilocalyx are grown primarily for their striking foliage. Plants grow upright to about 1 foot high. Leaves are crinkly, dark green with red undersides. Flowers are pale yellow. Some available species include *N. bullatus, N. forgetti, N. lynchii, N. melittifolius* and *N. cataractarum.* Native to South America.

Neomortonia
Flowers are similar to those of *Episcia,* but rose color. Leaves are small, ovate, light green, thick and bushy. A miniature type does well in terrariums.

Petrocosmea
These plants are similar to African violets. Flowers are white, creamy yellow or purple. Native to China, Burma and Thailand.

Alloplectus nummularis

Gesneria pedicellaris

Glossary

Anther
Expanded, yellow tip of the stamen, borne on a stalk or filament. It consists of one or more lobes that contain pollen. See Stamen.

Boy-Type Leaf
Leaf that is plain with smooth, non-serrated edges. Name derived from 'Blue Boy', which has this kind of leaf.

Calyx
Outer and lower floral lobes. Outside is green. Inside, called the *corolla*, is composed of colored petals.

Chromosomes
Microscopic bodies in the cells of any living thing. They carry characteristics of plant—bloom color, leaf size and shape—which are transmitted to new plants. See Gene.

Corolla
Part of flower that is formed by petals.

Crown
Main section of plant from which new growth emerges. Crowns can sometimes be divided to make more plants.

Cross-Pollination
Transfer of pollen from anthers of flower of one plant to stigma of flower on another plant.

Cutting
Leaf and stem removed from plant for purposes of propagation.

Disbudding
Removing buds to force blossoms to bloom at a particular time, such as for a show.

Division
Method of propagation where the plant crown is separated to make two or more plants.

Dominant Gene
Hereditary trait in genetic makeup of plant. Dominates recessive gene to determine plant characteristics. See Recessive Gene.

Floriferousness
Quantity of bloom on a plant.

Gene
A microscopic molecule or component of a molecule within the chromosome. It carries permanent traits that are transmitted to plants.

Germination
Sprouting of plants from seeds.

Girl-Type Leaf
Leaf that has a white spot at base. Named after 'Blue Girl', which has this kind of leaf.

Hybrid
Cross of two different plants to create a new, different plant.

Inorganic Fertilizer
Fertilizer manufactured from non-living sources, such as chemical salts.

Leach
Pouring quantities of water through soil mix in a container. Leaching washes away salts that accumulate in soil.

Leaf Mosaic
A term used in judging African violets in shows. Leaves have little overlapping and spaces between them.

Lobe
Petal of a flower.

Medium
Material in which plant roots are planted. Mediums include soil, perlite, vermiculite, sphagnum peat moss, sand or combinations of materials. Most African violets are grown in commercially prepared mix that is a blend of several ingredients.

Midrib
Central vein of leaf. Midrib of African violet leaves appears to be an extension of the *petiole*—the leaf stem.

Mutant
Plant that has certain, obvious differences from its parents. Mutants derive from changes in genetic structure caused by nature, not from hybridizing.

Organic Fertilizer
Fertilizer composed of once-living matter, such as fish emulsion. See Inorganic Fertilizer.

Ovary
Part of reproductive system of African violets. Can often be seen as slightly enlarged growth just beneath flower petals.

Ovules
Immature seeds contained in the ovaries.

Petiole
Stalk or stem of the leaf.

Pistil
Seed-bearing organ of flower consisting of ovary, style and stigma.

Pollen
Yellow, fertile, sperm-bearing particles released from the anthers.

Propagate
Multiplying plants by different means. Common methods of propagating African violets include rooting cuttings in soil or water, and starting plants from seeds.

Recessive Gene
Hereditary trait in genetic makeup of plant. Dominant genes control which characteristics will appear in new plants, so recessive traits are not usually visible in offspring. Recessive traits may appear in future generations.

Rootbound, Potbound—Growth of plant roots becomes restricted in pot. Roots begin to coil and tangle, filling the pot.

Sepal
Part of the calyx, a green cup that surrounds the colored petals.

Serrated
Edges of leaves are notched or toothed, much like a saw.

Soil pH
Level of acidity or alkalinity of soil. All plants have a preference. African violets prefer a soil that is slightly acid—6.4 to 7.0.

Stamen
Male organ of the flower. It produces and contains pollen. Consists of a stalk or filament topped by a lobe or lobes—the anthers.

Stigma
Part of the *pistil*—female part of the flower. Stigma is found at top of style. It receives the grains of pollen. Pollen travels to ovary where it can fertilize *ovules*—immature seeds.

Style
Part of female reproductive system in a flower. It is a slender projection from the ovary, topped by the stigma.

Sucker
Growth from crown of plant. Can be removed and planted to make a new plant.

Variegated
Variance in color, usually in reference to leaves. Color difference often appears in spots, streaks or along leaf edges.

Mail-Order Sources

The African Violet Company
399 Floral Ave.
Greenwood, SC 29647
Specialists in Optimara African violets. Carries full line of growing accessories. Free 16-page color catalog.

Annalee Violetry
29-50 214th Place
Bayside, NY 11360
Specialists in new varieties of African violets. Also carries selected gesneriads. Send 50¢ for variety list.

Buell's Greenhouses
Eastford, CT 06242
African violets and gesneriads. Large selection of gloxinias.

DiB's African Violets
Doris I. Bearman
918 Maple St.
Albion, MI 49224
Hybridizers of the DiB series. Write for descriptive list.

DoDe's Gardens
1490 Saturn St.
Merritt Island, FL 32952
Fertilizers, pest-control products and growing aids. Send self-addressed, stamped envelope (two stamps) for catalog of products.

Fischer Greenhouses
Oak Ave.
Linwood, NJ 08221
Large selection of African violets and other gesneriads. Send 25¢ for 16-page color catalog. Catalog of growing aids is available for $1.00.

Gesneria
Weynand Greenhouse
309 Montauk Highway
East Moriches, NY 11940
African violets and other gesneriads.

Hortense's African Violets
12406 Alexandria St.
San Antonio, TX 78233
Standards, compact standards, miniatures and semiminiature African violets. Send 25¢ for complete list.

Indoor Garden Supplies
Box 4056G
Detroit, MI 48240
Plant stands, carts, light fixtures, lamps, pots, meters and other accessories. Catalog free.

Kartuz Greenhouses
1408 Sunset Drive
Vista, CA 92083
African violets, gesneriads, begonias and other flowering house plants. Catalog $1.00.

Lyndon Lyon Greenhouses
14 Mutchler St.
Dolgeville, NY 13329
Specialists in African violets and other gesneriads. Many plants available at greenhouse that are not listed in the catalog. Send 50¢ for color catalog.

Mary's African Violets
19788 San Juan
Detroit, MI 48221
Carries growing aids, including large selection of soil mixes, amendments and fertilizers.

Nadeau Saintpaulia Seed Company
48 Queensbrook Place
St. Louis, MO 63132
Large selection of African violet seeds and seed-starting materials.

George W. Park Seed Co.
Greenwood, SC 29646
African violets are discussed on five pages in seasonal catalogs. Seeds of popular gesneriads are also available. All catalogs are free.

J. A. Peterson Sons
3132 McHenry Ave.
Cincinnati, OH 45211
Wholesale growers and shippers.

Tinari Greenhouses
2325 Valley Road
Box 190
Huntingdon Valley, PA 19006
Wide selection of African violets. Some accessories. Color catalog 35¢.

Quality Violet House
Route 3, Box 820
Walkerton, IN 46574
African violets, *Aeschynanthus* and *Columneas*.

The Violet House
Box 1274
Gainsville, FL 32601
Pots, potting materials, fertilizers, watering devices and related supplies.

Violets c/o Cookie
2400 Knightway Drive
Gretna, LA 70053
African violets. Send self-addressed, stamped, business-size envelope for complete list.

Zaca Vista Nursery
1190 Alamo Pintado Road
Solvang, CA 93463
African violets—starter leaves and plants. Catalog describes more than 850 African violets. Cost is $1.00, refundable with order.

Societies

African Violet Society of America Inc.
Box 1326
Knoxville, TN 37901
Membership $9.00 per year. Includes subscription to *African Violet Magazine*, published five times a year.

American Gloxinia and Gesneriad Society Inc.
Box 493
Beverly Farms, MA 01915
Membership $10.00 per year. Family membership $11.00. Life membership $150.00. Membership includes subscription to *The Gloxinian*, published six times a year.

Saintpaulia International
Box 549
Knoxville, TN 37901
Membership $7.00 per year. Includes subscription to *Gesneriad Saintpaulia News*, published six times a year.

Gesneriad Society International
Box 549
Knoxville, TN 37901
Membership $7.00 per year. Gesneriad Society International is an independent society, but has the same publication as Saintpaulia International: *Gesneriad Saintpaulia News*. Dues include subscription to this magazine, published six times a year.

Index

A

Achimenes, 36, 114, 115, 116
Acidity, 10
Aeschynanthus, 36, 113, 117, 118
Africa, 6
African violet basics, 9-33
African violet relatives, 113
African violet seeds, 40
African violet shows, 53
African Violet Society of America, 42
African violet soil mix, 10, 11
African violets, encyclopedia, 55
African violets, miniatures, 108-109
African violets, origin of, 6
African violets, propagation, 36
African violets, semiminiature, 108-109
African violets, standard, 57-107
African violets, trailing, 110-111
Agalmyla, 36, 138
Air circulation, 25
Air pollution, 17
Alkalinity, 10
Alloplectus, 36, 138
Altitude, 17
Anatomy, flower, 42
Anther, 41, 42, 140
Aphids, 30
Artificial light, 17, 18, 19
Asteranthera, 138

B

Baron von Saint Paul, 6
Bellonia, 138
Benlate, 32
Benomyl, 32
Besleria, 138
Bisexual, 41
Blackflies, 30
Bloom color, 55
Bloom shape, 55
Bloom type, 55
Botrytis blight, 32, 33
Bottle garden, 48, 49
Bottom watering, 9, 20, 21
Boy-type leaf, 140
Briggsia, 138
Broad mite, 30
Bulb pots, 9
Buying plants, 56

C

Calyx, 140
Cape primrose, 136
Capillary mats, 21, 22, 24
Captan, 32
Chemicals, safety, 29
Chirita, 36, 138
Cholorophyll, 16
Chromosomes, 41, 140
Clay pots, 13, 14

Codonanthe, 36, 138
Collecting plants, 36
Color spectrum, 17
Columnea, 36, 113, 119, 120, 121
Containers, 13, 35
   for propagation, 35
Controls, pests and diseases, 32
Cornell *Smithiantha* hybrids, 134
Corolla, 140
Crown rot, 32, 33
Crowns, 39, 140
Cross-pollination, 140
Cultural problems, 32, 33
Cuttings, 140
Cyclamen mite, 30
Cygon, 32
Cythion, 32

D

Daytime temperatures, recommended, 23
Dicofol, 32
Dimethoate, 32
Disbudding, 52, 140
Diseases, 28, 32, 33
Displaying African violets, 45-49
Division, propagation, 39, 140
Dominant traits, 41, 140

E

Electric humidifiers, 24
Encyclopedia of African violets, 55
Episcia, 36, 113, 122, 123, 124
Exposures in the home, 16, 17

F

Ferbam, 32
Fertilizer, 9, 26-27
   burn, 21
   salts, 27
Fish emulsion, 26
Flame violet, 122
Flats, 35
Floriferousness, 50, 140
Flower anatomy, 42, 140
Fluorescent light, 7, 16, 17, 18
   cool-white, 18
   intensity, 19
   two-tube fixture, 18
   warm-white, 18
   wide spectrum, 18
Foliar feeding, 27

G

Gas leaks in the home, 25
Gene, 41, 140
Germination, 140
Gesneria, 36, 138
Gesneriaceae, 5
Gesneriads, 5, 113-139
   lesser-known, 138
   propagation chart, 36

Gesneria pedicellaris, 139
Girl-type leaf, 140
Glass gardens, 48
Glazed pots, 13
Glossary of terms, 140
Gloxinia, 7, 36, 113, 128, 129, 131, 132
   numbered varieties, 133
Goldfish plant, 119
Granulated fertilizers, 27
Gray-mold blight, 32
Grooming guidelines for African violets, 52
Growth habit, 56

H

Hermann Wendland, 6
Homemade soil mixes, 10
Home temperatures, 23
Home troublespots, 25
Horticultural vermiculite, 11
House-plant potting soil, 12
Humidity, 9, 23
   how to increase, 15, 24, 37
   trays, 23, 24
Hybrid, 140
Hybridizing, 41-43
Hygrometer, 23

I

Incandescent light, 18
Inorganic fertilizer, 26, 140
Insect pests, 30, 31

K

Kelthane, 32
Koellikeria, 36, 138
Kohleria, 36, 113, 125, 126

L

Latitude, 17
Leach, 27, 28, 140
Leaf color, 56
Leaf cuttings, 36, 37, 38
Leaf mealy bug, 30
Leaf mosaic, 140
Leaf rib, propagating, 130
Leaf rot, 21
Leaf shape, 56
Leaf type, 56
Leaves, adjusting for symmetry, 51
Light, 16-19
   plant growth, 18
   requirements of plants, 9
   too little, 18
   too much, 18
Liquid fertilizers, 27
Lobe, 140

M

Magic flower, 114
Mail-order plants, 36

Mail-order sources, 141
Malathion, 32
Medium, planting, 10, 140
Midrib, 140
Miniature African violets, 48, 108-109
   'Betcha', 108
   'Joyful', 108
   'Love Bug', 109
   'Wee Hope', 109
Miniature landscapes, 48
Miniature *Sinningia,* 129
Miniature *Smithiantha,* 134
Misting to increase humidity, 24
Mites, 30
Mutant, 6, 140

N
Natural fertilizers, 26
Nautilocalyx, 36, 138
Nematanthus, 36, 113, 127
Neomortonia, 36, 138
New plantlets, 37
Nighttime temperatures,
   recommended, 23
Nut orchid, 114
Nutrients, 26

O
Organic fertilizer, 26, 140
Organic matter, 10
Orthocide, 32
Ovary, 41, 140
Overfertilizing, 26
Overwatering, 20
Ovules, 41, 140

P
Pan-type pots, 9
Pasteurizing mixes, 12
Patented varieties, 55
Peacock plant, 122
Perfect plants, 41
Perlite, 11
Pests and diseases, 28-33
   controls, 32
Petiole, 140
Petiole rot, 32, 33, 119
Petrocosmea, 36, 138
pH, 10
Photosynthesis, 16
Pistil, 41, 140
Plant displays, 45
Plant growth and light, 18
Plant-growth lights, 18
Plant problems, 28-33
Planting mediums, 10, 35
Plastic pots, 13, 14
Pollen, 41, 140
Pollinating flowers by hand, 43
Pot within a pot, 14

Pots and potting, 13-15, 29
   clay, 13
   drainage holes, 13
   plastic, 13
   potting step by step, 15
Powdered fertilizers, 27
Powdery mildew, 32, 33
Problems, preventing, 29
Propagation, 35-40, 140
   division, 39
   leaf cuttings, 123
   leaf rib, 130
   seeds, 40, 123
   stolons, 123
   suckers, 39

Q
Quarantine, 28

R
Recessive traits, 41, 140
Red spider mite, 30
Replanting, 15
Rest period, 125
Rhizomes, 36, 125
Ring spot, 32, 33
Rootbound, 14, 15, 140
Rooting hormone powder, 37
Rooting leaf cuttings in soil mix, 37
Rooting leaf cuttings in water, 38
Root nematodes, 30
Root system, 14
Rosette of plant, 51
Royal Botanical Garden, 6

S
Saintpaulia, 5, 36
Saintpaulia ionantha, 6
Sanitation, 28
Scale insects, 30
Scaly rhizomes, 114
Seeds, 36
   propagation, 40
Semiminiature African violets, 55,
   108-109
Sepal, 42, 140
Serrated leaf, 140
Shade trees, 17
Shipping plants, 36
Showing African violets, 50-53
   judging, 50, 51
Sinningia, 36, 129, 131
   standard, 130
Slipper plant, 129
Smithiantha, 36, 113, 134, 135
   hybrids, Cornell, 134
   miniature, 134
Societies, 140
Soil, 10-12
   drainage, 10
   homemade mix, 10

   pasteurized, 10, 11
   plant growth, 11
   pH, 10
   soilless mixes, 10, 11, 12, 119
   sterilized, 10
   texture, 10
Soil mealy bug, 30
Springtails, 30
Stamen, 41, 140
Standard African violets, 55, 57-107
   'Alabama' Optimara, 57
   'Alberta' Optimara, 57
   'Amazen Grace', 58
   'Anna' Ballet, 58
   'Arizona I' Optimara, 59
   'Arizona II' Optimara, 59
   'Arkansas' Optimara, 60
   'Artist's Dream', 60
   'Atlanta' Optimara, 61
   'Barbara' Rhapsodie, 61
   'Berry Splash', 62
   'Blue Border', 62
   'Blue Fandango', 63
   'Blue Tempest', 63
   'Calais', 64
   'California' Optimara, 64
   'Cameo Queen', 65
   'Candy Cane', 65
   'Carla' Ballet, 66
   'Claret Queen', 66
   'Colorado' Optimara, 67
   'Confessions', 67
   'Connecticut' Optimara, 68
   'Coral Radiance', 68
   'Crater Lake' Optimara, 69
   'Delaware' Optimara, 69
   'Dolly' Ballet, 70
   'Double Uncle Bob', 70
   'Eileen's Pink', 71
   'Erica' Ballet, 71
   'Evelyn' Rhapsodie, 72
   'Fantasy Royal', 72
   'Frosted Finesse', 73
   'Garnet Elf', 73
   'Georgia' Optimara, 74
   'Glacier' Optimara, 74
   'Grace' Ballet, 75
   'Hawaii' Optimara, 75
   'Heidi' Ballet, 76
   'Helga' Ballet, 76
   'Illinois' Optimara, 77
   'Indiana' Optimara, 77
   'Jazzberry Pink', 78
   'Josie', 78
   'Juliana', 79
   'Juliana' Rhapsodie, 79
   'Kansas' Optimara, 80
   'Kentucky' Optimara, 80
   'Leila's Blue', 81

'Light Giant', 81
'Lisa' Ballet, 82
'Louisiana' Optimara, 82
'Lucy' Rhapsodie, 83
'Manitoba' Optimara, 83
'Margit' Rhapsodie, 84
'Mark Mahogany', 84
'Marta' Ballet, 85
'Maryland' Optimara, 85
'Massachusetts' Optimara, 86
'Meta' Ballet, 86
'Michelle' Rhapsodie, 87
'Ms. Pretty', 87
'My Desire', 88
'Nashville' Optimara, 88
'Nebraska' Optimara, 89
'Nevada' Optimara, 89
'New Brunswick' Optimara, 90
'New Jersey' Optimara, 90
'New Mexico' Optimara, 91
'North Carolina' Optimara, 91
'Ohio' Optimara, 92
'Oklahoma' Optimara, 92
'Ontario' Optimara, 93
'Pamela', Rhapsodie, 93
'Pink Pippin', 94
'Pink Ulli' Ballet, 94
'Plum Frostee', 95
'Pom Pom Delight', 95
'Rhode Island' Optimara, 96
'Rio Rita', 96
'Rosana' Rhapsodie, 97
'Royal Ruby', 97
'San Francisco' Optimara, 98
'Sherbet', 98
'Smoky Mountains' Optimara, 99

'Snow Drift', 99
'Sophia' Rhapsodie, 100
'South Dakota' Optimara, 100
'Sparkle Plenty', 101
'Summer Lightning', 101
'Swan Lake' Ballet, 102
'Tawny Rose', 102
'Tennessee' Optimara, 103
'Texas' Optimara, 103
'Unspoken', 104
'Utah' Optimara, 104
'Vanessa' Rhapsodie, 105
'Venetian Lace', 105
'Washington' Optimara, 106
'Wisconsin' Optimara, 106
'Wrangler's Stampede', 107
'Wyoming' Optimara, 107
Standard *Sinningias,* 130
Stem cuttings, 36
Stigma, 41, 140
Stolons, 36, 122, 123
Streptocarpus, 36, 113, 136, 137
    Bavarian Belle 'Rexii' hybrids, 137
Style, 41, 42, 140
Suckers, 52, 140
    propagation, 39
Sulfur, 32
Sun and exposures, 16

T
Tablet fertilizers, 27
Tanzania, 6, 23
Temperatures, 9, 23
    changes and effect on plants, 23
Temple bells, 134
Thermometers, 19

Threadflower, 127
Thrips, 31
Time-release fertilizers, 27
Tools, 9
Top watering, 20, 21
Trace elements, 26
Trailing African violets, 55, 110-111
    'Buckeye Trails', 110
    'Snowy Trail', 110
    'Trails Delight', 111
    'Winding Trail', 111
Training plants for shows, 50
Transplanting, 14, 15
    seedlings, 40
Transporting plants, 52
Trunk, 14
Tubers, 36

U
Unglazed pots, 13

V
Vacationizing plants, 22
Variegated, 140
Ventilation, 23, 25
Vertical displays, 49

W
Watering, 9, 20-22
    methods, 21
    when you're away, 22
    wick, 20, 21, 22
Water-soluble fertilizer, 26, 27
Whiteflies, 31
Wide-spectrum fluorescent tubes, 18
Widow's tear, 114
Windowsill, 46

5.723653579017